the Water that Divides

Baptism Debate

Donald Bridge
& David Phypers

InterVarsity Press
Downers Grove
Illinois 60515

In writing and preparing this book
for publication our thanks are particularly
due to the Principal and the Librarian
of St John's College, Nottingham,
for making the facilities of the College
Library available to us. We have
also received invaluable help from Rev.
Dr Ernest A. Payne, formerly General
Secretary of the Baptist Union of
Great Britain and Ireland, in the writing
of chapters five and six. Last, but
not least, we are deeply grateful
to Mr Albert Phypers for his careful
proof-reading of the printed text and for
his compilation of the Index.

Needless to say we remain solely
responsible for all the opinions expressed
in the book and for any errors which
may inadvertently remain.

Also by Donald Bridge and David Phypers
Spiritual Gifts and the Church

First American printing, November 1977,
by InterVarsity Press, Downers Grove,
Illinois, with permission from Universities and
Colleges Christian Fellowship,
Leicester, England.

InterVarsity Press is the book publishing
division of Inter-Varsity Christian Fellowship,
a student movement active on campus
at hundreds of universities, colleges and
schools of nursing. For information about local
and regional activities, write IVCF, 233
Langdon St., Madison, WI 53703.

Distributed in Canada through InterVarsity Press,
745 Mount Pleasant Rd., Toronto, M4S 2N5.

ISBN 0-87784-787-8
Library of Congress Catalog Card Number: 77-006029

Printed in the United States of America

Introduction *7*

Part I Baptism & Scripture

1 Baptism in the New Testament *15*
2 The paedobaptist approach *33*
3 The baptist approach *55*

Part II Baptism & History

4 After the apostles *73*
5 Medieval underground *86*
6 Reformation tragedy *95*
7 Mennonites and Calvinists *113*
8 The politician and the pot-mender *125*
9 Two centuries *137*
10 The missionary movements *143*

Part III Baptism Today

11 Problems for paedobaptists *153*
12 Problems for baptists *164*
13 The real issues *180*
14 Towards tomorrow *188*

Select bibliography 205

Index 207

Introduction

One of our Lord's last recorded commands to his followers was, 'Go . . . and make disciples of all nations, *baptizing* them in the name of the Father and of the Son and of the Holy Spirit' (Mt. 28:19). That his followers have, in general, obeyed his command is beyond question. With the rare exception of groups like the Quakers and the Salvation Army, Christians of all traditions, denominations and persuasions have baptized, and have regarded baptism as the means of entry into the church. Yet despite this, perhaps no command of Christ has occasioned so much controversy, division, bitterness and mistrust as this one. Indeed, as we shall show later, at times it has caused Christians to destroy each other with a ferocity, cruelty and hatred strangely at variance with him who constantly exhorted his disciples to 'love one another' (Jn. 15:12, 17).

Today, thankfully, persecution between Christians has largely ceased. Christians no longer ill-treat one another over baptismal differences. But that does not mean that we can ignore such differences. For it is precisely the situation of the church in this decade that causes the baptismal issue to surface with embarrassing and urgent regularity.

Imagine a modern young man whose early religious pathway has been a typical one of baptism in infancy, sporadic attendance at Sunday school in childhood, and a tearless parting from the church in his teenage years in favour of the more alluring interests of motor-cycle, girl-friend and disco. Then he meets vital Christianity for the first time. He is intrigued, impressed, troubled and eventually convinced. Christ becomes a reality. Life takes on new meaning. After a while he finds in baptism a rite tailor-made to express his new convictions. But what is this? His vicar is horrified. His new Christian friends are embarrassed. A Baptist minister down the road offers him baptism, or is it (whisper the word) rebaptism? Already, the Christian community which he was beginning to love and trust appears to be divided. He must make a decision which he is ill-equipped to make, and which bewilderingly presents itself as a matter of group loyalty. What is he to do?

Here is quite a different problem. Middle-aged parents with growing children move into a new area. They are life-long evangelicals, used to taking pride in the fact that faith transcends denominational barriers. Bible conventions and evangelistic crusades, youth camps and united Weeks of Prayer have all underlined this fact, and if truth be told, these parents are just a little bit derisive about the 'ecu-maniacs' who want to merge the denominations and their structures. 'We already have spiritual unity! We are all one in Christ Jesus!' they exclaim dismissively. But what is this? In their new neighbourhood they look anxiously for a church that will honour the Bible, proclaim the gospel in the power of the Holy Spirit, provide teaching and attractive fellowship for their offspring. The name on the notice-board matters little. Yet after finding such a church and attending for some time, they ask for membership – and the difficulties begin! The Baptist church demands that they be rebaptized. It is no longer enough to welcome them as brother and sister in Christ. The parish church requires confirmation. To be born again is not enough after all. If conscience forbids either of these, there is an odd arrangement called 'associate membership'. It does not appear in the New Testament, and that is not surprising, for it prevents them from fulfilling their New Testament role as limbs of the Body of Christ. They can 'join', but not hold office. They can 'take communion', but not exercise their spiritual gifts.

A third example is common. Two Christians decide to marry. They come from different denominational churches, but they met at college in the cheerfully eclectic atmosphere of the Christian Union. Obviously they must settle for membership of one church, so one of them graciously steps down and offers to join the other's denomination. Splendid! Unfortunately, the wife (let us say) who has taken the humble place must now be humbled still further. Her husband, it seems, was initiated the right way, but she got it wrong. She must retrace her steps and be rebaptized or confirmed (whichever it is), contrary to her own convictions, for the sake of the family.

A fourth example is the saddest. The family are unabashed pagans, one and all. They hold the religion of the average Englishman, the belief that there may well be a God somewhere, but, as little is known about him, all that is required is to be as decent as the next man and kind to old ladies. A new baby arrives. Custom suggests (and grandmother insists) that something religious should be done. The vicar is called in. Presumably he sits in his vicarage waiting for little tasks like this, for this is his job. For a few precious moments the Christian church is touching the circle of interests of those it rarely reaches. But in the event, how pathetic is the occasion! The family stand apprehensively around the font at the back of an empty church. Hands are shaken with the vicar, and the party hurries home. Grandparents are satisfied, mother a little misty-eyed, father confirmed in his half-formed theory that religion has got nothing whatever to do with real life. Years later, if the growing child stumbles across some evangelistic activity and is prompted to ask, 'Mummy, am I a Christian?' he receives the indignant reply, 'Of course you are! You were baptized, weren't you?'

All of these sad stories illustrate the fact that controversy about baptism is far from being an academic luxury for arm-chair theologians. The witness of the church when it touches the unconverted, and the unity of the church when it welcomes the converted, are both at stake.

It is not the authors' intention to write a book settling the baptismal controversy. After two thousand years of varying tradition and understanding, that would be impossible. But it is their conviction that Christians should face the issues fairly and squarely, and should learn to live together in understanding and not in ignorance of their differences. It will not do to overlook their divisions and concentrate on 'preaching the gospel', as evangelicals have tended to do during the present century, for as Pierre Marcel[1] (a paedobaptist) and G. R. Beasley-Murray[2] (a baptist) both cogently insist, each from scriptural premises, preaching the gospel involves preaching about baptism.

Hence we shall begin by looking at New Testament references to Christian baptism and drawing conclusions from them. Next we shall concentrate on elucidating the reasons why some Christians believe that adult converts and their children should be baptized, while others are willing to baptize adult converts only. Thirdly, we shall attempt to show how this particular controversy arose in history, with particular emphasis on the Reformation and Puritan periods. Finally, we shall summarize and make practical suggestions whereby, in a mobile society, Christians might succeed in worshipping and working together in one community while preserving their cherished beliefs and traditions.

[1] Marcel, *The biblical doctrine of infant baptism* (James Clarke, 1953), pp. 135, 136.

[2] Beasley-Murray, *Baptism today and tomorrow* (Macmillan, 1966), p. 96.

Throughout the book the word *paedobaptist* will be used to describe those who accept the validity and necessity of baptizing infants and little children incapable of conscious faith. The word *baptist* (with a small b) will describe all others who insist on the need for conscious faith to precede baptism. Such baptists are not necessarily adult baptists. Most are willing to baptize young teenagers. Many, particularly in the United States, will baptize children as young as six or seven, but they still insist on a conscious confession of faith first. Not all baptists (with a small b) are Baptists (with a capital B); baptist belief extends far beyond specifically-named Baptist churches and denominations.

Part I

Baptism & Scripture

1
Baptism in the New Testament

The reader of the New Testament is confronted immediately with baptism. To avoid it, he would have to ignore the events surrounding the beginning of Christ's ministry and the beginning of the church's life. For the first public appearance of Jesus was heralded by John's baptism; the first public act of Jesus was to be baptized; and the first evangelistic sermon of the infant church was climaxed by a mass-baptism.

These facts promptly raise questions to which scholars have given much attention. How much was John's baptism borrowed from popular Jewish customs? Why did Jesus submit to baptism? How much development was there between the simple rite recorded in Acts and the theological significance given to it in Paul's Epistles? A full enquiry is quite beyond the scope of this book,[1] but every Christian should at least be aware of the more obvious scriptural references.

The baptism of John

Mark's Gospel gives us the fullest account of the significance of John's baptism, while some additional material is

[1] For an excellent account of the issues involved see Beasley-Murray, *Baptism in the New Testament* (Macmillan, 1963), chs. 1–4.

provided by the other Evangelists. First, says Mark, 'John the baptizer appeared in the wilderness, preaching a baptism of repentance. . . .' (Mk. 1:4). People who came to John for baptism therefore needed to be conscious of failure and of guilt. They needed to be sufficiently concerned about it to abandon certain kinds of behaviour. They had to show a practical desire for a better way of life. Significantly, John's most scathing words were reserved for those who sought his baptism without fulfilling these conditions. The Pharisees and Sadducees, the religious and political leaders of the Jews, were told to 'bear fruit that befits repentance' (Mt. 3:8). The enthusiastic crowds in general were warned that more was involved than a moving ceremony and some revivalistic excitement: selfishness should give way to generosity, dishonesty to fairness, bullying to kindness and grumbling to gratitude (see Lk. 3:7–14).

Secondly, John's message spoke of what God gives as well as what he demands. Those who were baptized not only expressed their sorrow for past misdeeds, but also echoed their joyful discovery that God was willing to wipe the slate clean. So, as they confessed their sins (Mk. 1:5) they looked backward to failure, forward to amendment and upward for forgiveness. These elements of confession, repentance and forgiveness were the main features of John's baptism as underlined by Mark's account.

Matthew, however, tells us more. John's baptism had an eschatological element, that is, it was concerned with 'the last days', with a turning point in history, with a climactic moment in God's dealings with mankind. It was because the kingdom of heaven was 'at hand' that John issued his call (Mt. 3:2). It was from 'the wrath to come' that men needed to flee (Mt. 3:7). 'Even now', said John, 'the axe is laid to the root of the trees' (Mt. 3:10). For this reason the people must repent and be baptized.

The Christian reader, wise after the event, can see how

right John was. A crisis more intense than his hearers could imagine was upon them. All of their national history had been moving towards this moment. The purpose hidden in God's heart before creation, was about to be unfolded. The Christ who was God's unique provision and mankind's only hope, was about to burst upon the scene. Their reaction to these events would reveal their inmost motives and either condemn them or bring them into the sweep of God's plan, in which nothing could ever be the same again.

For this reason, all of the Evangelists agree that John's baptism was incomplete and that he acknowledged the fact. 'I baptize you with water for repentance,' he proclaimed, 'but he who is coming after me . . . will baptize you with the Holy Spirit and with fire' (Mt. 3:11; see also Lk. 3:16; Mk. 1:8; Jn. 1:33). The people needed John's baptism, they needed to confess and repent of their sins, they needed to accept God's forgiveness, but when they had done all this they must not think that God had finished with them. John's baptism was but a preparation for another baptism, baptism with the Holy Spirit, and only the Coming One would be able to give that.

Jesus' baptism

To the baptism of John came Jesus, and despite John's protestation was baptized by him in the River Jordan (Mt. 3:13–17; see also Mk. 1:9–11; Lk. 3:21, 22; Jn. 1:29–34). Why? Why did Jesus join the ranks of those who flocked to John's baptism? He had no sins to confess, nor sins of which to repent and be forgiven; for although in every respect he has been tempted as we are, 'yet', says the writer to the Hebrews, this was 'without sinning' (Heb. 4:15). Jesus answered John's hesitation by saying, 'Let it be so now; for thus it is fitting for us to fulfil all righteousness' (Mt. 3:15), but what does this mean? The answers have been many and various.[1] Perhaps an answer may lie in comparing Jesus' answer to John with Isaiah 53 and Hebrews 2. Isaiah 53 paints a picture of a suffering Messiah, 'despised and rejected . . . a man of sorrows, and acquainted with grief' (verse 3). 'He has borne our griefs and carried our sorrows . . . he was wounded for our transgressions, he was bruised for our iniquities' (verses 4, 5). Hebrews 2 takes up the same theme. Identifying Jesus with the Messiah, the writer says, 'since therefore the children share in flesh and blood, he himself likewise *partook of the same nature*, that through death he might destroy him who has the power of death. . . . Therefore he had to be made like his brethren *in every respect*, so that he might become a merciful and faithful high priest. . . . For because he himself *has suffered* and been tempted, he is able to help those who are tempted' (verses 14, 17, 18). Jesus was not a sinner, but in order to save sinners according to the purpose of God, he had to take his place alongside sinners, becoming, to the casual observer at least, completely indistinguishable from them. This he consistently did, and was often misunderstood as a result. To people who equated religion with a strict separation from certain open misdeeds and a critical attitude towards the less scrupulous, the relationship of Jesus with all kinds of people was a continual puzzle. He did not seem to be particular about the company he kept; he seemed to like joining in parties; he offered friendship to undesirable characters; he clothed religious conceptions in shockingly homely speech. He sat loose to the many regulations that normally pushed a devout man out of the company of others. 'This man receives sinners and eats with them,' they complained (Lk. 15:2). To such an attitude misunderstanding was inevitable, for to some a man is judged by the company he keeps. Yet to a ministry marked by the attitude of Jesus, acceptance of John's

[1] See Beasley-Murray, *Baptism in the New Testament*, pp. 45–66, for an invaluable summary and discussion of these.

baptism was a suitable prelude, for in that baptism he was associating himself with sinners. More than that, he was identifying himself with their situation. So complete was that identification that its climax was reached in his death when, hanging between two thieves on a cross prepared for a third, 'he himself bore our sins in his body on the tree' (1 Pet. 2:24).

How then did Jesus' baptism 'fulfil all righteousness'? For Jesus, as for everybody, righteousness was submission to the will of God. For Jesus in particular, that meant accepting the task of providing salvation for those who turn to God. By insisting on baptism at the hands of John, Jesus was taking a decisive step of submission and humiliation in a process which began at Bethlehem and was to end at Calvary, in obedience to the Father's wishes. How appropriate, then, that that obedience should be recognized by his father; that 'when he came up out of the water, immediately he saw the heavens opened and the Spirit descending upon him like a dove; and a voice came from heaven, "Thou art my beloved Son; with thee I am well pleased"' (Mk. 1:10, 11)! So Jesus' Messianic work commenced. The Spirit was given to aid him in his task while the Father testified his good pleasure in him who 'did not count equality with God a thing to be grasped, but emptied himself. . . .' (Phil. 2:6, 7).

Christian baptism

Christian baptism was first administered on the Day of Pentecost and its similarity to John's baptism is immediately apparent. 'Repent, and be baptized' commanded Peter when his audience was 'cut to the heart' (Acts 2:37, 38). 'Be baptized . . . in the name of Jesus Christ for the forgiveness of your sins,' he continued (Acts 2:38). Thus far there is little difference in his message from John's. Christian baptism, like John's baptism, is a sign and means of repentance and forgiveness. But, of course, Christian baptism is more. John had foreseen and foretold baptism in the Holy Spirit, and this Peter now promised to his hearers. 'Repent . . . and be baptized . . . and you shall receive the gift of the Holy Spirit' (Acts 2:38).

This connection between water-baptism and Spirit-baptism recurs throughout the Acts of the Apostles. Thus Ananias went to see Saul in Damascus that he might regain his sight and *be filled with the Holy Spirit.* And after Saul had regained his sight 'he rose and was baptized' (Acts 9:17, 18). Similarly, at the house of Cornelius, after the Holy Spirit had been poured out, Peter declared, ' "Can any one forbid water for baptizing these people who have received the Holy Spirit just as we have?" And he commanded them to be baptized' (Acts 10:45–48). Yet again, after baptizing the twelve men at Ephesus, Paul laid hands on them and the Holy Spirit came upon them (see Acts 19:5, 6).

The same connection between baptism and the Holy Spirit is taken up in the Epistles. 'For by one Spirit we were all baptized into one body,' writes Paul, 'and all were made to drink of one Spirit' (1 Cor. 12:13), and again, in his letter to Titus he speaks in the same breath of 'the washing of regeneration and renewal in the Holy Spirit' (see Tit. 3:5–7). In addition to these explicit references, G. W. H. Lampe has concluded that when Paul speaks of 'the seal of the Spirit' (see *e.g.* 2 Cor. 1:22; Eph. 1:13; 4:30) he is referring to his readers' water-baptism.[1]

This direct equation between baptism and reception of the Holy Spirit cannot be stressed too strongly. Throughout Christian history, many have separated the two, using the idea of a post-baptism baptism of the Spirit to justify the practice of confirmation, while in the present century pentecostal teaching has made a similar separation though on rather different grounds from earlier teaching. Yet in the light of the New Testament such a separation is hard to

[1] Lampe, *The seal of the Spirit* (SPCK, 1967).

justify. Baptism in water and baptism in the Spirit are indeed logically separate events, and each is possible without the other. The Samaritans in Acts 8 were baptized in water without being baptized in the Spirit. The Romans in Acts 10 were baptized in the Spirit without being baptized in water. But theologically the two belong to each other. They are different aspects of one great initiation complex which includes the *inward attitudes* of repentance and faith, the *outward marks* of water-baptism and the laying-on of hands, and the *declaration by God* of sin's forgiveness and heart renewal. The subjective enjoyment of these things may well be delayed or disconnected. It is possible to be forgiven and not to feel clean. It is possible to be inwardly renewed and yet not to be joyfully and liberatingly conscious of it. It is possible to be incompletely aware of what God has given, or to be aware of it but to neglect it. It is possible to be ill-instructed about God's gifts, or emotionally unable to enjoy them fully. But surely since the Day of Pentecost to which John pointed forward, there is no need deliberately to separate water-baptism and Spirit-baptism, nor does New Testament teaching do so.

Besides demonstrating the Christian's reception of the Holy Spirit, baptism in the New Testament also demonstrates the fact that salvation is all of God's grace. Writing to Titus, Paul declares, 'when the goodness and loving kindness of God our Saviour appeared, he saved us, not because of deeds done by us in righteousness, but in virtue of his own mercy, by the washing of regeneration. . . .' (Tit. 3:4, 5). Grace is an absolutely fundamental word in the New Testament. It speaks of the favour and kindness which God extends to men and women utterly regardless of their condition or their deserts. It can never be said too strongly that God's love for us has nothing at all to do with our being lovable or even likeable. His love for a depraved and disgusting renegade whom he is calling back to himself is the same in quantity and quality as his love for a new-born babe who has had no opportunity to break the laws of God or men. This is very hard for human beings to grasp, because however much we use the word grace, in actual fact we cannot break free from ideas of love which connect it with merit and approval. Persistently we fall back into ideas of earning God's grace and of putting him in our debt, forgetting that such expressions are a contradiction in terms. So one will seek to grasp God's love and salvation by moral earnestness, another by religious observance, another by sensibly 'deciding for Christ'. But 'by grace you have been saved through faith; and this is not your own doing, it is the gift of God' (Eph. 2:8). Since baptism is a declaration of the gospel, it is an announcement of God's grace: the emphasis, as in Paul's words to Titus, is on God's coming to us, not on our doing something for him.

This gracious salvation is appropriated by faith, and baptism declares this too. When the Samaritans believed Philip as he preached good news about the kingdom of God and the name of Jesus Christ, they were baptized (Acts 8:12). When the Ethiopian eunuch asked Philip, 'What is to prevent my being baptized?' an early addition to the text of Acts regarded as authentic by many New Testament scholars tells us that Philip replied, 'If you believe with all your heart, you may.' And the eunuch replied, 'I believe that Jesus Christ is the Son of God.' Then Philip baptized him (see Acts 8:36–38 with footnote). When the Philippian gaoler asked Paul and Silas, 'What must I do to be saved?' Paul replied, 'Believe in the Lord Jesus, and you will be saved, you and your household.' And he was baptized at once, with all his family (see Acts 16:30–33). When Paul preached in Corinth 'many of the Corinthians hearing Paul believed and were baptized' (Acts 18:8). And when Paul wrote to the Colossians he declared, 'you were buried with him in baptism, in which you were also raised with him *through faith* in the working of God. . . .' (Col. 2:12). In the New Testament faith and baptism are always intimately connected, each being held to complement the other.

In addition to all this, in two of the most important of all New Testament passages on the meaning of baptism (Rom. 6:1–4; Col. 2:12 ff.), Paul stresses the connection between baptism and the Christian's participation in the death and resurrection of Christ. Coming to Christ involves dying and rising with him and there is no more vivid reminder of this than the act of baptism. Entering the water the Christian shares in Christ's death ('we were *buried* ... with him by baptism into death', Rom. 6:4; 'you were *buried* with him in baptism', Col. 2:12): leaving the water he shares in his resurrection ('in which you were also raised with him', Col. 2:12). In dying with Christ the Christian dies to sin. He accepts God's forgiveness secured on the cross (see Col. 2:14) and his old self is crucified with Christ that his sinful body might be destroyed and he might no longer be enslaved to sin (see Rom. 6:6). In rising with Christ the Christian becomes alive to God (Rom. 6:11). The life he henceforth lives he lives to God (Rom. 6:10). Death and sin no longer have dominion over him (see Rom. 6:9, 14).

This fundamental change from death to life which occurs in a person's life when he comes to Christ is called elsewhere in the New Testament, 'being born anew' (see Jn. 3; 1 Pet. 1:3) and its representation in baptism causes Paul to speak of 'the washing of regeneration and renewal' (Tit. 3:5). While the New Testament insists that regeneration must involve a personal response to the claims of Christ, it also makes clear that, having been born anew, the Christian cannot and must not continue to live in isolation from others, for once regenerate, the Christian becomes a member of the people of God, the church. Thus baptism in the New Testament is portrayed as the means of entry into the Christian church. Thus Paul writes, 'by one Spirit we were all baptized into one body' (1 Cor. 12:13). To be baptized without belonging to the church is a contradiction in New Testament terms. The three thousand who were baptized on the Day of Pentecost 'devoted themselves to the apostles' teaching and fellowship, to the breaking of bread and the prayers' (Acts 2:42) and these were corporate not individual activities.

Finally, and once again like John's baptism, Christian baptism in the New Testament has an eschatological element. It is concerned with the last days. Paul speaks of 'the washing of regeneration . . . so that we might . . . become heirs . . . of eternal life' (Tit. 3:5–7). He who is baptized thus looks to the future. Already alive to God, he looks beyond the grave to the perfect life when sin and sorrow will be no more and he will live and reign with Christ for ever.

Symbol or sacrament?

In view of Scripture's apparently clear teaching on the meaning and significance of baptism some readers might find it strange to realize that Christians have differed very sharply on their understanding of the value and importance of the rite. Is baptism merely a symbol, a vivid picture of what takes place in a person's life when he comes to Christ, or is it more? Is baptism a sacrament, a means of grace whereby God gives to the baptized something which he withholds from the unbaptized? In Roman Catholic and Orthodox thought baptism is quite clearly a sacrament. It is a sacrament in the sense that it brings salvation and entry into the church by its very administration without any response being necessary in the life of the one who is baptized. It works, of itself, whenever it is received. As a Catholic once explained succinctly to one of the authors: 'God's grace is kept in a box. Only by living in the box can you receive the grace. The box is the Church. Baptism puts you in the box.'

Support for this extreme sacramental understanding of baptism is found particularly in the words of Jesus to Nicodemus: 'Truly, truly, I say to you, unless one is born of water and the Spirit, he cannot enter the kingdom of God' (Jn. 3:5). Baptism, it is claimed, is obviously in Jesus' mind, and his insistence on baptism as necessary for entrance into the kingdom of heaven thus gives it its sacramental quality. To reason thus, of course, is to isolate one text from the whole of its New Testament context. Baptism, as has been shown, is the sign and seal of the whole process of regeneration, which in turn involves confession of sin, repentance, faith and quickening of the Spirit. Baptism, as will be shown, may indeed be necessary as part of the obedience of faith, but this is not to say that baptism, indiscriminately administered, automatically conveys salvation as a wire may automatically convey electricity when it is joined to positive and negative terminals. Jesus' words in John 3 must surely be understood in the light of the rest of the New Testament where no automatic understanding of baptism can be found. Furthermore, *if* baptism is as absolutely necessary to salvation as its sacramental advocates maintain, how could the dying thief have been saved – yet before he died Jesus promised him a place in Paradise (Lk. 23:43)?

The sacramental view of baptism held by Roman Catholic and Orthodox Christians helps to explain the importance attached by them to paedobaptism. Infants and little children are baptized that they may be saved and escape the flames of hell. Baptismal water must be at hand whenever a child is born lest in the early critical moments of life he expire and be lost for evermore. While normally desirable that the priest should baptize, when death is at hand, anyone may baptize and save a soul for eternity.

Against such crude sacramentalism the Reformers, with their emphasis on justification by faith alone, naturally and rightly reacted. But did they go too far? In their abhorrence of the magical and superstitious respect for baptism held by many of the common people, did they minimize the meaning of baptism and accord it less importance and significance than it is granted by the New Testament? Baptists traditionally came to see baptism as nothing more than a beautiful picture of the change which comes in the individual's life when he is converted and comes to Christ. They asserted that their mode of administration, by immersion, graphically depicted the believer's dying and rising with Christ, but what was really important was not his baptism, but his faith. It was faith and faith alone which saved. Make baptism a means of grace of value in itself and the way would be opened back to all the magic and crude superstition of pre-Reformation times. Baptists, however, were not the only Christians to insist on the exclusively symbolic nature of baptism. Similar ideas were adopted by some who, after the Reformation, continued to hold to paedobaptism as well. Since it was faith that saved, and not baptism, paedobaptism could be no more than a picture of the salvation which the infant might one day receive on his personal confession of faith. But beyond the fact that the baptized infant would enjoy a Christian home, a Christian education and the prayers of the church, he was basically no better off in the sight of God than the unbaptized infant, and a child did not need to be baptized in order to be brought up in a Christian home, taught in a Christian atmosphere and enjoy the prayers of other Christians for his salvation. What was really important for the infant, however, was not whether or not he was baptized, but that in due time he should believe in order to be saved.

Now undoubtedly, baptism is symbolic. The cleansing property of water makes it particularly suitable to represent the cleansing from sin which comes with conversion. Particularly when administered by immersion, but basically no less so when administered by sprinkling or pouring, baptism does vividly portray the individual's dying and rising with Christ as described in Romans 6 and Colossians 2. The trouble is, when baptism is viewed as a symbol and nothing more, its importance gradually decreases. If baptism is not necessary to salvation why bother to be baptized? Its insistence on penitence and faith *alone* as necessary for salvation has enabled the Salvation Army to dispense with baptism altogether, while among some baptists the situation is not all that dissimilar.[1]

Surely however, the close association between baptism and every element of salvation in the New Testament, as outlined above, makes it abundantly clear that, besides being a symbol, baptism is also a sacrament, a means of God's grace. When Peter was asked on the Day of Pentecost, 'Brethren, what shall we do?' he did not reply, 'Repent and believe . . . for forgiveness . . . and the Holy Spirit.' He replied, 'Repent, *and be baptized*' (see Acts 2:37–39). When Paul wrote to the Corinthians about their place in the church he did not write, 'By one Spirit we were all received by affirmation of faith into one body.' He wrote, 'By one Spirit *we were all baptized* into one body' (1 Cor. 12:13). When Peter wrote to a group of Christians who probably were about to be baptized or who had just been baptized he did not write, 'Faith saves you.' He wrote, 'Baptism . . . saves you' (1 Pet. 3:21). To the New Testament writers there is no problem. Baptism is integral to the salvation process, of value in itself, bringing with it the full blessing of God on the Christian.

Now of course, faith saves, and in asserting that baptism is a sacrament as well as a symbol, there is no suggestion that Christians should return to the crudely superstitious position of the Middle Ages. Where there is faith without baptism for one reason or another, there is still salvation and eternal security. The dying thief was not baptized but he was promised a place in Paradise (Lk. 23:43). Thus Christians who die unbaptized will still enter the kingdom

[1] See Beasley-Murray, *Baptism today and tomorrow*, ch. 4.

of heaven. Little children who die unbaptized will inherit the kingdom, for 'to such belongs the kingdom of heaven' (Mt. 19:14).[1] But in the New Testament baptism and faith together constitute the individual's response to God. When the Corinthians heard Paul preach many 'believed *and were baptized*'. Lydia saw her baptism as part of being 'faithful to the Lord' (Acts 16:15). Jesus said that making disciples involved baptizing them (Mt. 28:19), and the early church believed he also said that baptism was part of the obedience of faith (see Mk. 16:16). In the New Testament baptism without faith is dead, achieving nothing. Faith without baptism is incomplete, for through baptism God conveys to the believer all that is granted him in Christ.

Immersion, pouring or sprinkling?

Throughout Christian history baptism has been administered by immersion, by pouring and by sprinkling. At times Christians have differed passionately concerning the correctness of one method or another, even to the point of denying the validity of any form of baptism which differed from their own. Baptists have tended to insist on baptism by immersion as the only correct form. Some of them have asserted that this was the only kind of baptism practised in New Testament times and sometimes, as a result, they have been unwilling to recognize the validity of baptisms by pouring or sprinkling, even when those so baptized have fulfilled other conditions normally laid down for proper baptism.

Baptists reach their conclusions about immersion from the meaning of the Greek verb *baptizein* which means 'to immerse' and from the burial and resurrection symbolism of Romans 6 and Colossians 2. They claim that only a baptism by immersion in which the candidate is 'buried' in

[1] See John Pridmore, 'Of such is the kingdom', *Crusade*, August 1973, Thirty Press Ltd.

the water before rising from it can adequately fulfil this symbolism. Thus they claim that all New Testament baptisms were by immersion and that therefore any other form of baptism is at best imperfect and at worst invalid.

Few serious students of the New Testament would contest the claim that *baptizein* means 'to immerse' or the claim that baptism by immersion graphically depicts the idea of being buried and raised with Christ. Indeed many who baptize infants by sprinkling or pouring often baptize adults by immersion. On the other hand they may point out that there is no clear evidence on either theological or historical grounds that *all* New Testament baptisms were by immersion.

On theological grounds it may be claimed that pouring is as appropriate a form of baptism as immersion, in that it portrays the outpouring of the Holy Spirit on the believer, which is represented in baptism. In this connection Acts 10:44–48 might be adduced as particularly relevant for in this passage we read that Peter was amazed that the Holy Spirit was *poured out* even on the Gentiles, as a result of which he commanded them to be baptized. Does not the language perhaps suggest that the baptism of Cornelius and his household was a baptism by pouring and not immersion?

Equally it may be claimed that baptism by sprinkling represents the sprinkling with the blood of Christ which all Christians receive when in faith they lay hold of the benefits of Christ's death for themselves (see Heb. 12:24; 1 Pet. 1:2). Indeed, if the First Letter of Peter is a baptismal treatise as many have suggested, might not Peter's words, in the reference indicated, suggest that his readers had been baptized by sprinkling rather than by immersion?

In addition to all this, difficulties arise when actual accounts of baptisms in the New Testament are examined, for in several instances baptism by immersion would appear to have been impracticable if not impossible. Is it essential, for example, to suppose that on the Day of Pentecost the apostles baptized by immersion three thousand people in the forecourt of the Temple? How would the facilities be made available? It is hardly likely that the Temple authorities would permit unqualified laymen of a suspected movement to use the lavers provided for ceremonial washings inside the Temple. There may have been a procession down to the Pool of Siloam but certainly nothing is recorded of it. Of course, an argument from silence proves nothing, but we cannot conclude from the story that the mode must have been immersion, and there are factors which make it unlikely.

The incident in the home of Cornelius is another example. There may have been public baths in the military complex at Caesarea, and the converts could have been immersed there. But the 'feel' of the story gives the strong impression of an immediate baptism of the family and servants on the spot, and this, together with the theological symbolism, already noted, of the pouring out of the Spirit, suggests that baptism by affusion was much more likely.

Similar comments could be made about the account of the baptism of the Philippian gaoler and his family (Acts 16:33). Does the story really imply that the family, together with Paul and Silas bleeding from their flogging, trooped through the streets to the river in the early hours of the morning, in the aftermath of an earthquake, in order for the penitents to be immersed? The only water mentioned in the story is the few basinsful used to wash the evangelists' wounds; it would surely have been sufficient and peculiarly appropriate to have baptized by affusion with the same water.

Baptisms by immersion there certainly were in the New Testament, and very likely they were the most common. The Ethiopian eunuch was almost certainly immersed, for we read that both he and Philip 'went down into the water' and 'came up out of the water' (Acts 8:38, 39). Lydia and her household were probably immersed, for Paul preached to them by the riverside (Acts 16:12–15). And later, Paul drew lessons from the symbolic 'burial' of immersion, as has been seen. But equally he drew lessons from the symbolic 'putting off' of the candidates' old clothes and the 'putting on' of baptismal garments, in what are generally regarded as baptismal passages (Rom. 13:12–14; Col. 3:8–14). Yet it would be a rash person indeed who argued that a baptism was not valid if it was not preceded by undressing and dressing in order to provide the symbol. Surely an insistence on the precise detailed copying of the symbol lays the emphasis on the wrong place, namely on the symbol rather than the reality, on the type rather than the fulfilment, on the outward rather than the inward, and such an attitude is contrary to the whole spirit of the gospel.

Certainly there can be no clear scriptural reason for quarrelling about the mode of baptism, and there seems to be no reason why baptism should be delayed or abandoned because facilities for immersion are not available, or because delicacy, infirmity or old age make it inadvisable. Nor should Christians be made to feel that their own baptism is invalid or inferior merely because of the small amount of water used.

Believers only or their children as well?

While differences on the significance and form of baptism need not divide Christians, the problem of who is eligible for baptism is much more vexatious, and, as has already been stated, has been a source of deep division among Protestant Christians ever since the Reformation. Involved in the controversy are differences of opinion about the practice of the New Testament church, about the nature of the church itself, about the intrinsic status of children within the kingdom of heaven and about the scriptural doctrine of the covenant of grace. Also involved, and lamentably omitted by many writers on baptism, are the related practices of infant dedication among baptists, and confirmation among paedobaptists. The traditions of centuries, together with strengths and weaknesses in the arguments adduced by both sides, make a solution of the problem and reconciliation seemingly impossible. Yet in the post-Christian era Christians must learn to live together even though that may involve agreeing to disagree. It is our fervent hope that what is written in the following pages will increase understanding, remove suspicion, and help all Christians, whatever their persuasion, to maintain the unity of the Spirit in the bond of peace (Eph. 4:3).

2
The paedobaptist approach

Kumar was a student at university in the North of England. Brought up in East Africa as a Hindu, he was deeply impressed by members of his college Christian Union, and quietly committed his life to Christ. Before long he saw the need to be baptized. Even though he knew that this public profession of faith would bring upon him the grief and anger of his family, he determined to claim 'his high allegiance'.

Few Christians would doubt that he acted aright, though the cost was high. For all acknowledge that when an adult pagan or a member of any non-Christian religion is converted to Christ he should be baptized. On every continent, among Christians of every denomination, the baptism of such converts is a familiar and joyful sight. What is in dispute is the assertion that infants and little children should also be baptized. Some Christians would say that all infants (or as many as possible) should be baptized, others would restrict baptism to the infants of parents who request their baptism, while others would limit baptism to the infants of practising Christians. Discounting, for the moment, these differences of opinion about the extent of paedobaptism, what are the reasons these Christians advance to justify their position?

Historical evidence

a. The evidence of the Bible

Paedobaptism was obviously practised in the New Testament church, say its exponents, because we read on several occasions of whole families and households being baptized. When Lydia was converted 'she was baptized with her household' (Acts 16:15). When the Philippian gaoler heard the word of the Lord 'he was baptized at once, with all his family' (Acts 16:33). When Paul wrote to the Corinthians he recalled that he had baptized 'the household of Stephanas' (1 Cor. 1:16). Now, say paedobaptists, it is inconceivable that in these households there were no little children and infants. The text makes it abundantly clear that these were baptized along with their parents and other responsible members of the household. This would be fully in accord with the biblical view of family solidarity. Families were much more closely-knit than they are today in western society. We must imagine something more akin to a Jewish ghetto or a Hindu village than a modern British family. Decisions made by the head of the family directly and almost unquestioningly affected the rest of the members. Such households as those of Cornelius (Acts 11:14), Crispus (Acts 18:8) and Onesiphorus (2 Tim. 1:16) give examples of this principle in action. Thus, it is further asserted that, even if there were no infants in the families whose baptisms are explicitly recorded in the New Testament, infants born into these families would be baptized at birth, or shortly afterwards. So, it is concluded, paedobaptism is a thoroughly scriptural practice.

b. The evidence of the Fathers

What happened during the period following the apostles? By the early third century, Origen, an influential teacher, was writing, 'The Church has received a tradition from the Apostles to give baptism even to little children.'[1]

[1] Origen, *Commentary on Romans*, V.ix.3.

Clearly he believed this; presumably he had received baptism himself in infancy. Had his parents in turn? and his grandparents? So suggests the modern German scholar Joachim Jeremias.[1] If he is correct, it follows that paedobaptism was being practised at least as early as the beginning of the second century, very close to the New Testament period.

The example of Polycarp is even more impressive. In the year AD 156 persecution broke out against Christians in Asia Minor. Among those who died for their faith was the aged Polycarp, bishop of Smyrna. His death, dramatic and moving as it was, marked a watershed in the history of the early church, for he was its last living link with the apostles themselves, having been influenced by John. Paraded in the stadium and commanded to curse Christ, he gave the noble reply, 'Eighty-six years have I served him, and he has done me no wrong: how then can I blaspheme my King who saved me?'[2] Must he not be referring to his infant baptism eighty-six years before, and does not this imply that such baptism was therefore an apostolic practice?[3]

In similar vein, Justin Martyr, who wrote brilliantly in defence of Christianity, as a kind of second-century C. S. Lewis, referred to 'many men and women of the age of sixty and seventy years who have been disciples (or 'were made disciples') of Christ from childhood'.[4] This again dates childhood discipleship, and therefore (it is claimed) paedobaptism, as far back as late apostolic times.

[1] Jeremias, *Infant baptism in the first four centuries* (English translation: SCM, 1960), p. 66.

[2] *Letter of the church of Smyrna*, IX.3. Quoted in Stevenson, *A new Eusebius* (SPCK, 1960), p. 21.

[3] See *e.g.* Dix, *The theology of confirmation in relation to baptism* (Dacre Press, 1946), p. 31, footnote 2.

[4] Justin, *First apology*, 15.6.

c. The evidence of Jewish proselyte baptism

Admission to the Jewish faith can come in two ways: by birth and by conversion. Gentile converts to Judaism are called proselytes. When proselytes were admitted to the Jewish faith in biblical times they received certain ceremonial washings which may be described as baptism. Reference has already been made to the belief, current among many modern scholars, that Christian baptism, as it developed, was influenced by Jewish baptism.[1] Some scholars also believe that in certain circumstances the children of proselytes were baptized along with their parents, and, arguing from this premise, conclude that the children of Christian parents would have been baptized, in like manner, in the early church.

Of particular importance in this connection are Paul's words in 1 Corinthians 7:14. Addressing Christian partners of marriage where one partner was not a Christian he says, 'For the unbelieving husband is consecrated through his wife, and the unbelieving wife is consecrated through her husband. Otherwise, your children would be unclean, but as it is they are holy.' What does Paul mean? Is he not reflecting the Jewish idea that children born to proselytes before conversion to Judaism were born 'unclean' and were therefore baptized with their parents, while those born afterwards were 'born in holiness'? If he is, then this verse is claimed to provide further apostolic support for paedobaptism.

Theological evidence

Few paedobaptists leave the argument at the historical stage. They claim that there are strong theological reasons for the baptism of infants, which rest neither on isolated biblical texts nor on occasional historical references. The

[1] See above p. 15.

theological arguments invoked vary a good deal, and must now be outlined.

a. The nature of baptism itself

Reference has already been made to the view that baptism is of value in itself, bringing salvation merely by its administration, without any response of faith being necessary in its recipients. According to this position, baptism saves *ex opere operato*, that is, by the work being worked. In other words, the fact of the outward action produces the fact of the inward change. Thus, he who is baptized is saved, while he who remains unbaptized is lost. This idea developed quickly from about the time of Augustine (354–430), when the doctrine of original sin had become clearly formulated and widely accepted.

Starting from such scriptures as Romans 5:12–21 and 1 Corinthians 15:21, 22, Augustine maintained that every member of the human race is born both sinful by nature, and personally guilty, under the just condemnation of God. He attempted to explain this in terms of the organic unity of mankind by which the whole race existed seminally in Adam its head, and therefore shared with him in his first transgression. With various modifications this has been the orthodox belief of Christians ever since, and however difficult or even offensive it may sound to modern ears, no alternative has been offered which does justice to the facts of history and the words of the Apostle Paul.

What was really novel from the fifth century onwards was not the statement of this doctrine, but the link forged between this and the baptism of infants – a subject which of course nowhere appears in Paul's discussion of original sin. Newly-born babies were seen as being in danger of dying without hope of salvation *unless* they received baptism for the washing away of their original guilt. Augustine himself reasoned not from original sin to paedobaptism, but vice versa. In his gathering of evidence for a doctrine of sin which he knew to be offensive, he appealed to the already favoured practice of baptizing infants. His argument, in effect, went like this: The church baptizes babies, but baptism is for the remission of sins, and babies have not yet deliberately and intelligently chosen to sin. For what, then, do they need forgiveness? There is only one answer – for the offence they committed in Adam. Thus the doctrine of original sin is supported by the acknowledged custom of the church.

As an argument it was effective, but it was not an example of Augustine at his most biblical, and before long it was being used in the opposite direction to justify and explain paedobaptism. Augustine himself seems to have taught that baptism is the dividing line between babies who die lost and babies who die saved. Certainly this was the justification for paedobaptism advanced by the church of the Middle Ages. And although it may be expressed in less bald terms, such would no doubt be the position maintained by many Roman Catholic and Orthodox Christians at the present time.

However, quite apart from other arguments for or against paedobaptism, this can never be held by the Christian who takes the Bible as his yardstick. A view of forgiveness and salvation which sees it as automatically conferred or withheld must be rejected. A view which places the really critical emphasis not on the grace of God, or on the proclamation of the gospel, or on the response of faith, but pins everything to the performance of a ceremony, is completely alien to the spirit and letter of the New Testament. Wherever we place faith in relation to baptism, we cannot say that it has no part at all, and that is what this view ultimately does.

b. Jesus and children

Turning from this extreme sacramental view, those Protestants who nevertheless support the baptism of infants adopt quite different arguments. To begin with, many find support in Jesus' teaching about children, as recorded in the Gospels.

In Mark 10:13–16 we read, 'And they were bringing children to him, that he might touch them; and the disciples rebuked them. But when Jesus saw it he was indignant, and said to them, "Let the children come to me, do not hinder them; for to such belongs the kingdom of God. Truly, I say to you, whoever does not receive the kingdom of God like a child shall not enter it." And he took them in his arms and blessed them, laying his hands upon them.' Parallel passages are found in Matthew 18:3; 19:13–15 and Luke 18:15–17. The Lucan version is particularly significant, for it makes the point that some, if not all, of the children who were brought to Jesus were 'even infants', a different Greek word being used to describe them from the one translated 'children' in Matthew and Mark.

Admittedly, the reasoning goes, these passages are not concerned explicitly with baptism, but such are their implications that they make paedobaptism imperative. First, it is pointed out, Jesus was indignant with his disciples when they tried to turn the children away. Thus, baptists who refuse baptism to little children are as guilty as the disciples. Secondly, Jesus said that the kingdom of God belongs to children. Thirdly, the proper way for an adult to receive the kingdom is for him to emulate the child. If the kingdom of God belongs to children, and if the way to receive the kingdom is to receive it like a child, how dare we refuse children, even infants, the sacrament of the kingdom, namely baptism? Jesus did not baptize the children who were brought to him because he did not baptize, and in any case Christian baptism had not been instituted. But by laying his hands on them Jesus showed that none of the blessings of the kingdom were to be denied to children.

c. Baptism and salvation

For many, the teaching and example of Jesus in the Gospels is sufficient justification for the practice of baptizing little children. Others, however, find further support for their conduct in scriptural teaching on the nature of salvation and the grace of God.

Salvation, they say, is the work of God. It is an objective thing, begun, enacted and finished solely by God himself. It does not depend on the subjective response of man in faith, for that response, though necessary, is itself part of the work of God. To argue otherwise would be to make the response itself a 'work' which earns salvation. It is easy to reject the idea that salvation comes by self-effort, human decency or religious observance, and then slip into the suggestion that people are saved because they are sensitive enough or wise enough to respond to the offer of the gospel.

Because salvation is objective, the reasoning goes, adult baptism tends to emphasize the subjective response of the convert rather than the objective fact of God's grace. Paedobaptism, on the other hand, by being performed on those who cannot exercise conscious faith, more aptly portrays the objective nature of salvation and the necessity for the sovereignty of God in its execution.

In this connection it is often urged that in paedobaptism the *prevenient* grace of God is displayed. That is to say, God comes to us before we turn to him, as Jesus said to his disciples, 'You did not choose me, but I chose you....' (Jn. 15:16). In *Baptism in the New Testament* Oscar Cullmann has developed this idea. He sees the baptism of Christ as being the prototype of all subsequent Christian baptisms. When one is baptized one enters into the baptism of Christ. Thus all the benefits of Christ's baptism were in a special sense prevenient. Because the infant who is baptized enjoys all the benefits of his baptism *after* he has been baptized, paedobaptism is a particularly suitable vehicle to display this prevenient aspect of baptism.

Cullmann's ideas have been further developed and have found expression in official Church of Scotland reports of recent years:

'"Baptism" refers to the one all-inclusive vicarious baptism of Christ for all men; the once-and-for-all baptism of Christ in blood upon the cross and the once-and-for-all baptism of the church in Spirit at Pentecost are correlative, and so the baptism of Christ for all men can be spoken of as the baptism of the church. . . . When an individual is baptized within this church, he too is baptized into Christ who was born of the Spirit, who died and who rose again. That is why the baptism of children of Christian parents is so right that it is taken for granted in the New Testament.'[1]

'Common humanity is shared by every man and by Christ Himself . . . the one qualification for baptism is (Man's) membership in the sinful humanity which Christ has redeemed.'[2] Infants, just as much as adults, possess this qualification and thus should be baptized.

d. Baptism and the covenant of grace

The most persuasive and fundamental argument for paedobaptism has yet to be considered. It is based on an understanding of the covenant of grace as it is presented in the Bible. It is also the argument least understood by many who reject paedobaptism. Neither are its conclusions fully acceptable to all paedobaptists. Indeed, the line of reasoning has been largely the preserve of the Scottish and continental Reformed churches and their overseas offshoots which find their inspiration in the teachings of John Knox and John

[1] *Church of Scotland interim report of commission on baptism*, 1955, p. 10.
[2] *The biblical doctrine of baptism* (study document issued by Special Commission of the Church of Scotland, 1958), p. 42.

Calvin. The most persuasive modern exponent of the view is the French Reformed pastor Pierre Ch. Marcel with his boldly entitled work, *The biblical doctrine of infant baptism*. Only since the appearance of this book has the position been enthusiastically adopted by a growing number of evangelical Anglicans. Whatever the strength of the position may be it must be recognized that it was quite unknown before the Reformation and cannot be found in any form in any of the writings of the early Fathers. To the supporters of the view this merely demonstrates how quickly New Testament teaching on the subject was lost in the Graeco-Roman world of the early Christian era.

What then is the basis of this covenant teaching? The Bible is divided into two main sections, the Old Testament and the New Testament. Some translations call these sections, quite correctly, the Old Covenant and the New Covenant, for in this context the terms *testament* and *covenant* are synonymous. A covenant is a solemn, binding agreement with promises and obligations, entered into by two or more parties and often ratified by oaths and visible signs such as sacrifices and the exchange of tokens. Marriage is a good modern example of such a covenant. Two parties, the man and the woman, enter into a binding agreement with each other to live together as husband and wife. They make promises and accept obligations. Their agreement is ratified by the exchange of a ring or rings as visible tokens that the covenant has been properly entered into and will be observed.

Because the Bible is divided into the Old Covenant and the New Covenant it is commonly believed that it tells how God has made two covenants with men. The first covenant was concluded on Mount Sinai through Moses with the people of Israel (see Ex. 19, 20). In it God offered salvation in return for obedience to his law. This 'old covenant' was thus the covenant of law. The second covenant, the 'new covenant', was concluded at Calvary with all mankind through Christ. In it God offers salvation in return for faith in Christ as the mediator of the covenant. This is the covenant of grace. It is a covenant of grace (*i.e.* undeserved favour) because it delivers man from the obligations of the covenant of law which were too difficult for him to keep anyway, and offers him salvation through faith in the sacrifice of Christ by which his sins are forgiven and put away.

It is this common belief in two basic covenants which advocates of covenant theology in fact reject. The really basic covenant in the Bible is the *one covenant of grace*. It is found throughout the Old and New Testaments. It is always received by faith. The two halves of the Bible should be regarded not as records of separate covenants made by God with mankind, but as records of the way in which the one covenant was administered in two different ways, for necessary reasons.

Support for this view is found in the Old Testament record of the life of Abraham and of the covenant God made with him (Gn. 15:5) and renewed at various times in his life, and in the statement with respect to this covenant that, 'he believed the LORD; and he reckoned it to him as righteousness' (Gn. 15:6). This is the covenant of grace. It is referred to frequently by Paul in the New Testament. For example, Romans 4 is a careful argument in reply to Jewish opponents of the gospel of grace. They quoted Abraham, their original forefather, as a supreme example of justification by works. This is the basis on which God has acted from the beginning, they claimed (verses 1, 2). 'Nothing of the kind!' replies Paul. Abraham was justified by faith even before he was circumcised (verses 3–12). The basic promise made to Abraham was entirely dependent on God's grace (verses 13–22). Exactly the same applies to the Christian believer today (verses 23–25).

A similar passage in Galatians 3 takes the argument further. The covenant of grace made with Abraham is the primary source of all understanding of God's dealings with men (verses 7–9). The covenant at Sinai did not follow for another four hundred and thirty years (verses 15–18). Its purpose was not to contradict what God had already said, but, by driving men to experience the utter futility of trying to earn his favour and approval, to prepare them to receive what he freely offers (verses 19–22). It was a kind of parenthesis in God's dealings with men, suited to them in their spiritual infancy until they were ready to enter into the full benefit of his grace, 'our custodian until Christ came, that we might be justified by faith' (verse 24).

The writer of the Letter to the Hebrews makes the same point: the 'old covenant' is not by any means the original or the fundamental covenant. Rather it provided a symbol of the real thing, a shadowy foretaste of the full blessing which God wishes to grant (10:1). Both before its inception, however, and during its implementation, faith was the essential basis of man's relationship with God. And throughout the period of the 'old covenant', from Abel to Abraham, from Moses to David, Samuel and the prophets, examples abound of men and women who were 'well attested by their faith' (Heb. 11).

This approach to the covenant of grace is advanced by all Reformed theologians, whatever their view on baptism, but those who favour paedobaptism now draw certain conclusions. They point to an important principle which they find displayed whenever God makes a covenant with men. This is that *God includes their children in the blessings of the covenant.*

This principle is particularly clearly displayed in, for example, God's dealings with Noah. In his generation, Noah alone found favour in the eyes of the Lord (Gn. 6:8). Yet God did not save him alone from destruction, but his children and their wives as well. Why? Because this is the way God deals with those with whom he makes covenants: 'But I will establish my covenant with *thee* (singular); and thou shalt come into the ark, thou and thy sons, and thy wife, and thy sons' wives with thee' (Gn. 6:18, RV). And again, 'the LORD said unto Noah, Come *thou and all thy house* into the ark; for *thee* (singular) have I seen righteous before me in this generation' (Gn. 7:1, RV). Thus Noah's wife, Noah's three sons and their wives were spared the Flood, not because *they* were righteous but because *Noah* was righteous.

After the Flood when God promised Noah never so to destroy the world again the same principle is again displayed. 'Then God said to Noah and to his sons with him, "Behold, I establish my covenant with you *and your descendants after you* . . . that never again shall all flesh be cut off by the waters of a flood. . . ." And God said, "This is the sign of the covenant which I make between you and every living creature that is with you, for all future generations: I set my bow in the cloud" ' *etc.* (Gn. 9:8–13). The implications are clear. To this day the human race has survived destruction by deluge, not because it deserves or has earned such survival, but because of God's promises to Noah.

God's inclusion of children within the orbit of a covenant is particularly apparent in the account of his dealings with Abraham. 'I will establish my covenant between me and you *and your descendants after you throughout their generations* for an everlasting covenant, to be God to you *and to your descendants after you*' (Gn. 17:7). Indeed the principle is apparent throughout the Old Testament. On one occasion Moses told the Israelites, 'The LORD our God made a covenant with us in Horeb. Not with our fathers did the LORD make this covenant, *but with us*, who are all of us here alive this day' (Dt. 5:2, 3), yet these Israelites were the children of those to whom God had literally appeared, for their fathers had died during the forty years' wanderings in the desert. On another occasion Moses declared, 'the things that are revealed belong to us *and to our children* for ever' (Dt. 29:29). The Psalmist declared, 'the steadfast love of the LORD is from everlasting to everlasting, upon those who fear him, and his righteousness *to children's children*, to those who keep his covenant and remember to do his commandments' (Ps. 103:17, 18). Isaiah said, 'Fear not, O Jacob my servant . . . I will pour my Spirit upon your descendants, and my blessing on your offspring' (Is. 44:2, 3 ff.). And again, of the Messiah he said, 'And he will come to Zion as Redeemer, to those in Jacob who turn from transgression, says the LORD. And as for me, this is my covenant with them, says the LORD: my spirit which is upon you, and my words which I have put in your mouth, shall not depart out of your mouth, or out of the mouth *of your children*, or out of the mouth *of your children's children*, says the LORD, from this time forth and for evermore' (Is. 59:20, 21).

Indeed, so central to the Old Testament is this aspect of covenant theology that God's dealings with Israel cannot be understood without it. It is because of his covenant with Abraham *and his descendants* that God continues to deal graciously with a wayward and rebellious people. It is on the basis of a continuing covenant that God requires his people to obey his law: 'the things that are revealed belong to us and to our children for ever, *that we may do all the words of this law*' (Dt. 29:29). It is because the Israelites are God's covenant people that the prophets can plead so strongly with them to turn from their wickedness to their God. It is because children are within this covenant that they can be and are to be instructed in its terms and conditions (see *e.g.* Ex. 12:26, 27; 13:8, 14, 15; Dt. 6:20–25).

Moving into the New Testament, the same principle that God includes children in his covenant dealings with their parents is similarly found. On the Day of Pentecost Peter declared, 'The promise is to you *and to your children*' (Acts 2:39). The angel who appeared to Cornelius promised a message by which he would be saved *and all his household* (Acts 11:14). Paul announced to the Philippian gaoler, 'Believe in the Lord Jesus, and you will be saved, *you and your household*' (Acts 16:31). Christian wives with unbelieving husbands were comforted with the certainty that *their children* were holy (1 Cor. 7:14). Children in the churches at Ephesus and Colossae were addressed in the same breath as their parents (Eph. 6:1–3; Col. 3:20).

Thus, it is concluded, the covenant of grace is one, the same in both Old and New Testaments. It is a covenant of salvation by faith and also a covenant in which children share its blessings on account of their parents' faith. In the Old Testament the covenant looks forward to Christ, who is clearly foreshadowed, while in the New it looks back to him, but it is still one covenant. In both Testaments the covenant is administered by word and sacraments, and although the sacraments differ with the Testaments they correspond to each other and together with the word speak of Christ. Thus the Old Testament sacrament of initiation, circumcision, is matched in the New by baptism. Circumcision displays Christ, for Paul says, 'In him (*i.e.* Christ) also you were circumcised with a circumcision made without hands, by putting off the body of flesh in the circumcision of Christ' (Col. 2:11). Baptism corresponds to circumcision, for Paul goes on to say, 'and you were buried with him in baptism, in which you were also raised with him through faith in the working of God, who raised him from the dead' (Col. 2:12). Similarly, the Old Testament sacrament of Passover finds its New Testament equivalent in communion. Passover speaks of Christ, for Paul writes, 'Christ, our paschal lamb, has been sacrificed' (1 Cor. 5:7). Communion corresponds to Passover, for it is a sacrament of the new covenant in Christ's blood (see 1 Cor. 11:25). Needless to say the church in the New Testament corresponds to Israel in the Old, for the church is the Israel of God (Gal. 6:16).

Now, who was to be circumcised in the Old Testament? Two types of people: adult converts to the faith of Israel ('proselytes') and the male children of Israelite parents. For both types circumcision marked their entry into the people of God. To fail to be circumcised was to break God's covenant (Gn. 17:14). So baptism should now be administered to similar groups of people: adult converts to Christianity and the children of Christians. To fail to baptize either is to break God's covenant.

Thus the argument is complete. It is based on the unity of Scripture and the analogy of Scripture. This is the reason why there is no specific reference in the New Testament to the baptism of infants and little children. Jewish converts to Christianity would automatically have had their children baptized along with themselves. They would have needed a specific command to refrain from so doing, and such a command cannot be found in the pages of the New Testament. Indeed, say the advocates of this viewpoint, of far more significance than the absence in the New Testament of any example of paedobaptism, is the absence of any example of the baptism of an adult born of Christian parents. Such a baptism would demonstrate that the conditions of entry into the covenant of grace were changed between the Old and New Testaments. But, it is asserted, the conditions of entry were not changed. The paedobaptism issue is settled. The practice is thoroughly scriptural and incumbent on all godly Christian parents. There are, however, certain corollaries of this position, important in themselves, and to a consideration of these we must now briefly turn.

One corollary of the covenant-theological justification for paedobaptism, and indeed of the whole paedobaptist position, is that children, and consequently adults, may be members of the visible Christian church although devoid of conscious faith. Whatever the place of faith in paedobaptism, the children so baptized cannot consciously believe, yet in baptism they are admitted into the church. As they grow older they may still fail to believe, yet, because they are baptized they are members of the church. It is important to point this out, for the constitution of the church is precisely one of the major issues in the baptismal controversy.

Many theologians, of course, find no problem in the idea that members of the church may not be personally committed, believing Christians. Indeed, they would suggest that it is quite unrealistic to attempt, with the baptist and his stress on faith before baptism, to identify the visible church with those who believe. Such a task is impossible, for it involves the setting up of some as judges over other men's souls, and in practice this always proves hazardous to say the least. Nominal Christians there may be among those baptized in childhood, but then, so there are among those baptized as adults, as an analysis of members in any baptist church would show!

Not only is it unrealistic to demand faith before baptism, it is also unscriptural. Jesus said, 'Judge not, that you be not judged' (Mt. 7:1), yet, as has been shown, the baptist position involves just that. Furthermore, Paul records of the Jews, God's covenant people, that they 'all were baptized into Moses in the cloud and in the sea. . . . Nevertheless with most of them God was not pleased; for they were overthrown in the wilderness' (1 Cor. 10:2, 5). Between the Red Sea and the wilderness these Israelites were counted as members of the covenant people and received many of God's blessings to his people. Only later did their true position become apparent when God judged them. Indeed this is one of Paul's recurring themes. 'He is not a real Jew who is one outwardly, nor is true circumcision something external and physical. He is a Jew who is one inwardly, and real circumcision is a matter of the heart, spiritual and not literal. His praise is not from men but from God' (Rom. 2:28, 29). 'Not all who are descended from Israel belong to Israel, and not all are children of Abraham because they are his descendants' (Rom. 9:6, 7). Only those with faith who are chosen of God belong to the true Israel (see Rom. 9:32; 11:2). As it was with the nation of Israel so it is with the visible church. Many are called but few are chosen. Only God knows those who are his and he will vindicate them at the last day.

A second corollary of covenant theology as it applies to paedobaptism is that baptized children must be regarded as Christians until they give clear evidence by their lives to the contrary. Just because children have been baptized does not mean that they will always be Christians. As they grow up and learn the implications of the covenant to which they have been admitted from birth, they may decide to reject its terms and conditions and cut themselves off from God's people. This they have a perfect right and freedom to do. This the Israelites of old were always doing: hence God's rejection of them as a people (see Rom. 11:7–10). Similarly, might not New Testament warnings against apostasy, particularly those in the Letter to the Hebrews (see Heb. 2:1–3; 4:1, 2; 6:4–6; 10:26–29; 12:25), be written to warn Christians baptized in infancy against suffering a similar fate? Apostasy apart, however, the covenant of grace and the administration of baptism to the children of Christian parents give to those parents the comfort and assurance that their children belong to God, that he loves them and cares for them and wills to bring them to salvation. The parents for their part, must observe the terms and conditions of the covenant particularly as these apply to children. They should train up their children in the way they should go, in the discipline and instruction of the Lord, that when they are old they will not depart from it (see Pr. 22:6; Eph. 6:4). Some indeed will depart from the way, but the majority will not, and while they are children, and until in adulthood they give clear evidence to the contrary, Christian parents can rest in the confidence that their children belong to Christ and are made regenerate by him.

A third corollary of covenant theology is that the Word of God should be preached in different ways to those baptized in infancy and those not so baptized. All men break God's covenant to some degree from time to time and need to repent and return to him. But those baptized in infancy need to repent, not that they might be admitted to God's covenant people, but because they already belong to that people.

After the Bathsheba affair, David pleaded with God for pardon 'according to thy steadfast love; according to thy abundant mercy' (Ps. 51:1). He prayed because he belonged to the covenant and he asked God to deal with him on its terms. When Peter preached on the Day of Pentecost he preached to the house of Israel and offered his audience repentance, baptism and the gift of the Holy Spirit because they were Israelites and thus members of the covenant people of God. When Paul preached at Lystra and at Athens (Acts 15:15–17; 17:22–31) he preached in quite a different way and commanded his audiences to repent from their idolatry that they might join the covenant people of God.

To suggest, of course, that the children of Christians are themselves Christians until they prove the contrary by rejecting the gospel, rather than assuming they are unbelievers until they profess faith, raises intriguing questions about the place of conversion in the Christian home, and about the unity of the gospel. Is there one gospel, for all, or are there two, one for the children of Christians and one for the children of non-Christians?

A fourth corollary of the covenant argument is that paedobaptism should only be administered in the context of 'discipline'. Baptism is not to be administered to all children because God loves all, or because Jesus blessed little ones, or because grace precedes faith; it is to be administered to certain children because they have certain parents. It requires in fact that some kind of 'judging' has to be done after all. In practice, it may be more difficult to decide who are truly Christian parents and whose children should therefore receive baptism, than it is to decide who are truly converted and should thus be baptized on that count.

Much space has been devoted to this particular argument for paedobaptism, because out of all those considered so far, it lays the greatest claim to over-all scriptural support, and because its weight (or even its existence) is not always recognized and understood by many who reject paedobaptism.

e. Baptism and faith

In chapter 1 reference was made to the close connection found in the New Testament between baptism and faith, so close in fact, that often the two terms are used synonymously when their effects are described. If faith is so necessary for baptism to be effective, it may be asked, how can a helpless infant exercise this faith, and how can it thus be right to baptize him? Three main answers have been given by paedobaptists to this question.

One answer, particularly associated with Martin Luther, has been that in the act of baptism faith is infused into the life of the infant. That such an idea is not foreign to Scripture is shown in the account of the birth of John the Baptist. Before John was born Mary went to visit his mother Elizabeth 'and she entered the house . . . and greeted Elizabeth. And when Elizabeth heard the greeting of Mary, the babe leaped in her womb . . . and she exclaimed with a loud cry, ". . . when the voice of your greeting came to my ears, the babe in my womb leaped for joy"' (Lk. 1:40–44). This passage shows, Luther claimed, that even before birth an infant can exercise faith. Just so, he concluded, in baptism faith can be present in the infant and the baptism can be truly Christian and scriptural.

This, of course, is extraordinary exegesis! Luther would have been on firmer ground had he based his reasoning on the promise in Luke 1:15 that John would 'be filled with the Holy Spirit, even from his mother's womb'. Thus even before birth an infant *can* be filled with the Holy Spirit.

A second answer is that the church baptizes children in view of coming faith. Faith is necessary for baptism to be effective, but there is nothing in Scripture to suggest that in baptism faith must always precede baptism. It may well follow later and when it does it will make the baptism just as effective as when it actually accompanies the sacrament.

A third answer is that in infant baptism faith is exercised by others on behalf of the child. These others may be the parents of the child and this view would particularly commend itself to those adopting the covenant theology approach to baptism. To these thinkers, parents, in baptizing their infants, exercise faith in the promises of God that their children are loved by him, are within his covenant and that he will bring them to ultimate salvation in Christ. That faith is not consciously exercised by the child at the moment of baptism does not matter. It is exercised in his place by his parents and thus in due time becomes effective.

Where parents are lacking in faith themselves, have died or have abandoned their child, then faith may be exercised by sponsors on behalf of the baptized. Along with, or in the absence of, the parents they make promises in his place and undertake to keep the terms of the covenant for him in matters of godly upbringing and discipline, that conscious faith on his part might later follow.

Along with parents and sponsors the church also exercises faith when an infant is baptized. It is into the church that the child is admitted, and the congregation, being present, welcomes him, promises to pray for him and to support his parents in his upbringing, and thus exercises its own faith that the child will, in due course, play an active part in its ranks.

These assertions that faith can be exercised by others on behalf of the child raise an important scriptural question – can one man's faith be effective for another, or must it always be his own faith that saves? Naturally, paedobaptists give the former answer to this question and instance the centurion's servant (Mt. 8:5–13), the paralytic borne by four (Mt. 9:1, 2), Jairus' daughter (Mt. 9:18, 23–26) and the epileptic boy at the foot of the mount of transfiguration (Mt. 17:14–21) as examples of children and adults healed and raised from the dead on account of the faith of others. As will be shown in the next chapter, baptists are not nearly so certain on this point, but the point is important and much of the case for paedobaptism hinges on its validity or otherwise.

These then are the main approaches employed by Christians to justify the practice of paedobaptism. Their whole position may usefully be summarized in the words of Calvin, 'If we would not maliciously obscure the kindness of God, let us present to him our infants, to whom he has assigned a place among his friends and family, that is, the members of the Church.'[1]

[1] Calvin, *Institutes*, IV.xviii.32.

3
The baptist approach

In contrast to the many lines of approach used by the advocates of paedobaptism, the baptist's approach is disarmingly simple. For him it is sufficient that, in his judgment, every doctrinal statement about baptism in the New Testament presupposes that baptism will be administered to those who consciously believe in Christ, and that it will be the token of their faith in him. For him it is decisive that every instance of baptism recorded in the New Testament is of men or women who have consciously believed in Christ and who thus wish to express their faith. For him, Philip's reply to the Ethiopian eunuch's question, 'What is to prevent my being baptized?' is paramount: 'If you believe with all your heart, you may' (see Acts 8:36 and footnote to verse 37).

Although it is recognized that the account of Philip's reply does not form part of the earliest extant manuscript of Acts, none the less baptists insist that the words of the reply reflect the universal yardstick of the apostolic church in administering baptism. That yardstick was conscious faith on the part of the baptismal candidate. If faith was present, baptism could proceed. If faith was absent, baptism must wait. In the words of Spurgeon, 'I consider that the "baptism" of an unconscious infant is just as foolish as the "baptism" of a ship or bell, for there is as much Scripture for the one as for the other.'[1] Consequently, baptists are quite unimpressed by the evidence outlined in the previous chapter in support of paedobaptism.

Historical evidence

Accounts of family and household baptisms in the New Testament have no bearing on the issue of paedobaptism, for a close examination of the narrative makes it quite clear to baptists that infants and little children were not included in these baptisms. Either there were no infants in the families concerned, or infants were specifically excluded from baptism because they were infants. Thus, if the promise to Cornelius (Acts 11:14) suggests that his infant children received baptism along with him, it is equally necessary to conclude that these same infants spoke in tongues and extolled God! (see Acts 10:46–48). If infant children were baptized along with the family of the Philippian gaoler they must have been brought from their beds in the small hours of the morning for the purpose! (see Acts 16:33). If Paul baptized infants in the household of Stephanas (1 Cor. 1:16) they must have been precocious infants indeed, for we later learn that 'the household of Stephanas . . . devoted themselves to the service of the saints' (1 Cor. 16:15). If infants were included in the baptism they must have shared in the service!

To the baptist, New Testament family baptisms do not illustrate the supposed scriptural idea of family solidarity, but merely record the fact that on the occasions mentioned whole families responded to the gospel. Thus, in the home of Cornelius 'the Holy Spirit fell on all who heard the word' (Acts 10:44). Those who were baptized in the home of the Philippian gaoler were the ones to whom Paul and Silas

[1] Spurgeon, *The early years: autobiography* (Banner of Truth, 1967), p. 149.

had previously spoken the word of the Lord (see Acts 16:32). At Corinth 'Crispus, the ruler of the synagogue, believed in the Lord, *together with* all his household' (Acts 18:8). Rather than exemplifying paedobaptism these passages would appear to deny it.

Indeed, many baptists are dubious about the whole idea of family solidarity in Scripture. In the New Testament Jesus warned of the possibly divisive effect that the Christian faith would have on families, rather than promising a cohesive effect: 'Do not think that I have come to bring peace on earth; I have not come to bring peace, but a sword. For I have come to set a man against his father, and a daughter against her mother, and a daughter-in-law against her mother-in-law; and a man's foes will be those of his own household' (Mt. 10:34–36). The Letters of Paul and Peter show how necessary this warning was, as they deal with the practical problems of families not united in faith (see 1 Cor. 7:1; 1 Pet. 3:1–6). Family solidarity in itself can thus provide no justification for paedobaptism.

Neither is the baptist impressed with evidence from the Fathers in support of paedobaptism. Origen's statement about its apostolic origin is very dubious when balanced against Tertullian's clearly-expressed doubts.[1] The argument from Polycarp's martyrdom founders on our ignorance of his age when he was martyred. His own words contain no explicit reference to baptism, only to serving Christ from an early age. As was shown earlier, baptists do not doubt that children can become Christians, and, strictly speaking, do not deny baptism to believing children.[2]

As for Jewish proselyte baptism, there is no evidence to prove that Christian baptism was influenced by it, and there is considerable doubt as to whether it even existed as early

[1] See ch. 4.
[2] See p. 11.

as the first century.[1] In this connection Paul's assertion that the children of a half-Christian family are 'holy' (1 Cor. 7:14) proves too much if it is used to support paedobaptism, for Paul also asserts that the unbelieving partner is similarly 'consecrated'. If the 'holy' children should be baptized, so should the 'consecrated' partners, yet this is a nonsense, for in the next breath Paul insists that these partners are 'unbelieving' and need to be saved (see 1 Cor. 7:15, 16).

It is the complete silence of the New Testament concerning any explicit reference to paedobaptism which settles the issue for the baptist. If he could find any shred of tangible evidence that the apostles baptized infants and little children then he would change his position, but until such evidence is produced he remains fixed in his belief that baptism should be given only to those who have consciously exercised faith in Christ and are thus determined to live for him.

Theological evidence

When baptists come to look behind the baptismal narratives of the New Testament to their theological significance, they are more firm than ever in their rejection of paedobaptism. Not only are they unimpressed by the arguments outlined in the previous chapter, they also find in Scripture a positive theology of the church, of salvation and of baptism which forbids them to baptize infants and insists on the baptism of conscious believers only.

a. The nature of baptism itself

Along with the majority of Protestant paedobaptists, baptists reject an *ex opere operato* view of baptism, which says that infants should be baptized to deliver them from the prospect of hell. Here baptists are completely at one with their Protestant brethren and reject all justification

[1] See Beasley-Murray, *Baptism in the New Testament*, pp. 18–30.

of any kind for baptism, for the reasons outlined earlier. Indeed, historically, so great has been the revulsion of baptists against the Catholic and Orthodox sacramentalist view of baptism that, until very recent years, few baptists have been willing to regard baptism as a sacrament at all, preferring to view it merely as an ordinance to be administered in obedience to our Lord's command.

b. Jesus and children

For baptists the Gospel passages about Jesus' reception of children (Mt. 18:3; 19:13–15; Mk. 10:13–16; Lk. 18:15–17) are irrelevant to the baptismal debate. First, the passages say nothing about baptism, nothing at all. They record an incident in the life of Jesus when he welcomed children, blessed them and said some important things about receiving the kingdom of God. But as Jesus said nothing about baptism, no conclusions about the rite can be deduced from the passages. Secondly, with the exception of Luke 18:15, the passages describe how *children*, not infants, were brought to Jesus, so even if conclusions about baptism *could* be drawn from them they would justify only child baptism, not infant baptism. In this connection care must be taken not to make too much of Luke 18:15. Two Evangelists out of three say children were brought to Jesus and all three agree that Jesus said, 'Let the *children* come to me' (see particularly Lk. 18:16). Even if infants were among those brought to Jesus the overwhelming majority were children old enough to *come* or turn away as they felt fit.

Thirdly, to justify paedobaptism from the passages in question would make nonsense of Jesus' related remarks about receiving the kingdom. In the first place these remarks were addressed to the disciples, to adults. It is adults whom Jesus finds it necessary to instruct in how to receive the kingdom, and that in itself is significant. Furthermore, receiving the kingdom is a conscious thing:

'whoever does not receive the kingdom of God like a child shall not enter it'; 'unless *you turn* and become like children, you will never enter the kingdom of heaven.' Infants can never be the example of adults in this, for infants are not capable of conscious choice. Finally, entering the kingdom of God involves humility and trust: 'whoever humbles himself like this child, he is the greatest in the kingdom of heaven.' This the child can effect more easily than the adult by virtue of his childlike character, but the child must still receive the kingdom in a way which an infant cannot do. Nothing in all this contradicts baptist theology, indeed it supports it. Entry into the kingdom comes through the exercise of conscious humble faith. Of this faith, baptism is the sacrament, and as such it is only to be administered in the context of conscious faith on the part of the one being baptized.

c. Baptism and salvation

With the assertions that God is the author of salvation and that his grace is operative in men's lives long before they consciously come to believe in him, most baptists would agree. But to conclude from this that infants should be baptized as a witness to the prevenient grace of God is, in the view of baptists, to commit a *non sequitur* of the highest order. Furthermore, if this *non sequitur* is then carried to its logical conclusion, it must lead to all the worst abuses ever associated with paedobaptism. If paedobaptism testifies to the prevenient grace of God then all infants must be baptized, for no-one can know in whom this grace will be fruitful in issuing in faith and salvation. Yet when infants are thus baptized indiscriminately the result is millions of baptized pagans, as in western Europe at the present time, and this is a scandal which is beginning to exercise some paedobaptists themselves.

That the prevenient grace of God is taught in Scripture is indisputable. But that is not the truth to which baptism bears witness. Baptism is a symbol of the equally important truth that grace demands and prompts the response of faith. Faith, for the baptist, is paramount. Baptism without conscious faith is not the baptism of the New Testament and is therefore condemned.

d. Baptism and the covenant of grace

As already suggested, it is when the covenant argument for paedobaptism is raised that differences in theology run most deeply. To make matters more confusing, baptists differ quite markedly among themselves in their response to this issue.

i. Baptists who reject covenant theology

Many baptists would reject out of hand the argument that Scripture reveals one covenant in Old and New Testament alike. They would see the most significant relationship between the two halves of the Bible as their discontinuity and their contrast. God, speaking through Jeremiah, they point out, promises a '*new covenant* . . . not like the covenant which I made with their fathers' (Je. 31:31, 32). Jesus, on the night of his betrayal, said, 'This cup is the *new covenant* in my blood' (1 Cor. 11:25). Paul, writing to the Galatians, makes a great deal of the *two* covenants (Gal. 4:24), and the author of the letter to the Hebrews builds a whole argument on the ministry of Christ 'as much more excellent than the old as *the covenant he mediates is better*, since it is enacted on better promises . . . therefore he is the mediator of a *new covenant*' (see chapters 8–10, particularly 8:6 and 9:15). The whole key to the Old Testament, it is maintained, is that at its centre was an imperfect and incomplete covenant, given in the wisdom of God to prepare the world for the coming of Christ; 'our custodian until Christ came' (Gal. 3:24).

In exact accordance with this fact, such baptists insist, the position of children in the New Testament is radically altered. Peter's pentecostal promise, 'to you and to your children', is qualified with the words, 'every one whom the Lord our God calls to him' (Acts 2:39). The context makes clear that that 'call' involves repentance and baptism, in that order. This is in accord with the general picture given throughout the New Testament, and it is precisely this which constitutes the difference between the two halves of the Bible. No longer do children enter a relationship with God on the grounds of natural birth into one select nation: now the grace of God is offered to people of all nations on the one condition of penitent faith. Many who thus respond will of course be children. They are addressed in Paul's letters (*e.g.* Eph. 6:1–3), not because they are the children of Christians, but because they are Christian believers themselves. Paul also assumes that there will be sad examples of Christians' children who will not believe, otherwise his insistence that elders, at any rate, should have believing families becomes meaningless (see Tit. 1:6).

To take up any other position, it is argued, would be to fly in the face of the whole trend of New Testament teaching. If Christians' children are born within the covenant of grace, how could Jesus insist that 'that which is born of the flesh is flesh' (Jn. 3:6), and 'unless one is born anew, he cannot see the kingdom of God' (Jn. 3:3)? How could John, commenting on these words, underline the stark distinction between being born of God and being born of human parentage (see Jn. 1:12, 13)? If a person is baptized in infancy, how can he in later life fail to be other than confused about his need for a personal encounter with God?

As for the argument from circumcision, this receives equally blunt rejection. It is true that circumcision was the mark of entry into the old covenant as baptism is the mark of entry into the new, but that in no way implies that the conditions applying to the administration of both are similar. Just the reverse is the case. The only New Testament reference in which the two are linked (Col. 2:11–14) cannot really be made to hold the implications given to it by paedobaptists, especially in view of clear warnings elsewhere. Paul asserts, for example, that true circumcision is not something external and physical, but is a matter of the heart, spiritual and not literal (see Rom. 2:28, 29). In other words, it is through his encounter with the crucified Saviour that the Christian has received his true circumcision. His life has been changed. Baptism singles out and underlines that fact: in it he has been buried and raised with Christ 'through faith in the working of God, who raised him from the dead' (Col. 2:12).

Paul's treatment of circumcision in his letter to the Galatians is even more emphatic. There he is fiercely combating the insistence of some Jewish Christians that Gentile converts should be circumcised. His reply is not simply that baptism has now replaced circumcision (how had the argument ever arisen if that was the simple equation?), but that faith responding to God's grace (expressed in baptism) has replaced commitment to legalistic effort (expressed in circumcision). If circumcision as a ceremony had the importance which covenant theologians give it, could Paul have written such words? And did the Apostle, demolishing false reliance on a ceremony thought to have saving power to whole families, proceed to replace it with another ceremony thought to do exactly the same? Clearly not! Circumcision and baptism are as different from each other as the covenants into which they mark entrance.

ii. Baptists who accept covenant theology

The approach to paedobaptism outlined above is typical of perhaps the majority of those who reject it; certainly of the majority who accept the denominational name of Baptist. However, baptist witness has always included a strongly Calvinistic tradition, and those who stand within that tradition obviously do not reject covenant theology. Yet they see no convincing reason for expressing such theology by baptizing infants. Their quarrel is not with the premise (one covenant of grace, accepted by faith, in Old and New Testaments), but with the conclusion (the automatic inclusion of all believers' children in that covenant). They argue bluntly that the paedobaptist has made a double mistake. He has allowed himself to be drawn into a church practice for which there is no specific command in the New Testament, and he has committed himself to a theory which is contradicted by specific New Testament statements, and even Old Testament teaching.[1]

The original covenant made with Abraham included two distinct elements, one physical and the other spiritual. For example, it promised a literal portion of land: 'I will give this land' (Gn. 12:7); yet it gave a foretaste of a spiritual inheritance: 'he looked forward to the city which has foundations, whose builder and maker is God', and, 'they desire a better country, that is, a heavenly one' (Heb. 11:10, 16). As Kingdon puts it, the covenant had both dispensational and transdispensational elements, the first fulfilled before Christ's coming, the second as a result of his coming.[2]

Thus, the word 'seed' or 'descendants' had a double meaning. Abraham's physical descendants would possess the land of Canaan (Gn. 12:7), but his spiritual descendants would be all those who would display a faith like his (see Rom. 4:16). Similarly, the rite of circumcision had two purposes: to mark out a special nationality ('the circumcised'), and to symbolize a moral and spiritual characteristic displayed only by some (as Moses and the prophets never tired of saying).

It is this distinction which the baptist maintains that the

[1] The two main contemporary exponents of this view in the English-speaking world are Paul King Jewett in *Infant baptism and confirmation* (unpublished), and David Kingdon in *Children of Abraham* (Henry E. Walter, 1973).

[2] Kingdon, *Children of Abraham*, p. 29.

paedobaptist has failed to recognize. Circumcision was the sacrament of a *national* group who were given a *physical* country, inherited by their *natural* offspring. For this reason it could be taken up into the national system given at Sinai. But it also symbolized the change of *heart* granted to people with *faith*. Therefore it was used in the covenant of grace, a covenant central to, yet also foretold in, the Old Testament, and brought to fruition in the New. In the New Testament, this covenant finds its fulfilment in the reality of new birth. The Christian equivalent of circumcision, therefore, is not baptism but regeneration. As Paul says, 'we are the true circumcision, who worship God *in spirit*, and glory in Christ Jesus' (Phil. 3 : 3), and, '*real circumcision* is a matter of *the heart*, spiritual and not literal' (Rom. 2:29).

What then of the promise made to 'your descendants' (Gn. 17:7)? This only applied to the natural descendants of Abraham during the dispensational period of the covenant. Transdispensationally, Abraham's descendants are those who display his faith. The promise is not that the children of Jews or the children of Christians are automatically included in the covenant, but that *there will always be a believing company*. It is as simple as that. There is nothing here of two ways of salvation, one by new birth, and the other via birth into a godly family. The New Testament references to families are simply particular applications of the universal message that whoever believes shall live. And, of course, whoever believes should be baptized; the symbol will then (and only then) correspond to the reality.

Having thus demonstrated that covenant theology does not lead to infant baptism, baptists who accept it can now join forces with those who reject it in their strictures against paedobaptist conclusions (as outlined above). Indeed, all baptists are at pains to stress that their position is much more positive than a simple denial of paedobaptist arguments. They assert that biblical teaching about the church, the gospel and the doctrine of baptism all support their position.

e. The doctrine of the church

Baptists often maintain that, in spite of their name, their distinctive doctrine is not that of baptism at all. They claim to be distinguished by their insistence that the New Testament knows only a church made up of professing believers. They find that faith is mentioned whenever entry into the church is in view.

Thus, on the Day of Pentecost, *those who received Peter's word* were baptized (Acts 2:41). After the healing of the man who sat at the Beautiful Gate of the Temple 'many of those who heard the word *believed*' (Acts 4:4). After the burial of Ananias and Sapphira and along with signs and wonders done by the hands of the apostles 'more than ever *believers* were added to the Lord' (Acts 5:14). After the appointment of the seven deacons 'the word of God increased; and the number of disciples multiplied greatly in Jerusalem, and a great many of the priests were *obedient to the faith*' (Acts 6:7). When the Samaritans *believed Philip* as he preached good news about the kingdom of God and the name of Jesus Christ, they were baptized, both men and women (Acts 8:12). This, say baptists, is the unchanging pattern of the New Testament. New Testament churches are composed of 'saints who are also *faithful* in Christ Jesus' (Eph. 1:1). This is the test which must be applied when baptism is requested: 'If you *believe* with all your heart, you may' (Acts 8:37, footnote).

A corollary of the baptist position is the concept of the 'gathered church'. Although this view is shared by some paedobaptists, it is fundamentally a baptist position. For him, for example, the church cannot be equated with a nation, for the people of a nation are too diverse to be all 'faithful brethren in Christ' (Col. 1:2). Neither can one belong to the church by virtue of one's place of birth, for that would deprive faith of its primary place in the economy of salvation.

This is the broader ground on which baptists base their position. It is the insistence that the Christian church is made up of Christians. 'Baptism for Baptists is a matter of churchmanship,' argues one of their best-known apologists. 'Because they have a high and holy conception of its membership, they feel that baptism should only be administered to those who understand its true significance and personally accept its solemn responsibilities.'[1] Writing to the bishops of the Church of England in 1926 Baptists maintained, 'We believe in the Catholic Church as the holy society of believers in our Lord Jesus Christ . . . we believe this holy society is truly to be found wherever companies of believers unite as churches on the ground of a confession of personal faith. . . . Because we hold the Church to be a community of Christian believers, the ordinance of Baptism is administered among us to those only who make a personal confession of repentance and faith.'[2]

This is the positive basis of the practice of baptism for adults only, and, whether or not it is accepted by all Christians, it deserves to be understood and respected by them. Its expounder is not a troublesome sectarian who denies that God loves children, but a churchman who believes that the church is not to be confounded either with the world or with its own sphere of influence within the world. He sees baptism as the door of the church, one that opens to receive believers and closes to exclude unbelievers. He suspects that once a Christian community begins to welcome the unbeliever, the half-believer and the infant incapable of belief within its actual membership, before three generations have passed that community will have lost its spiritual zeal and its evangelical experience as its distinctive Christian features fade.

[1] Cook, *What Baptists stand for* (Carey Kingsgate Press, 1947), p. 89.
[2] *The reply of the Baptist Union to the Lambeth appeal.*

f. The doctrine of salvation

All evangelical Christians insist that faith is the key to salvation. Justification by faith is the article of a standing or falling church, as Martin Luther declared. But the unregenerate human heart rebels against complete dependence upon God and longs to boast of earning its own favour with God. There is a constant tendency for the gospel of the grace of God to be muted, qualified and corrupted by additions which give sinful men the privilege of doing something for themselves instead of stretching out empty hands to God. The Christian must always be on guard against suggestions that his salvation partly depends on his own decency, his performance of religious efforts or his progress in personal morality. The New Testament is full of the danger, and church history traces its constant recurrence. 'By grace you have been saved through faith' (Eph. 2:8) is the consistent message of the Bible. When in the Bible baptism is sometimes linked with faith, it is clearly as an expression of that faith. Indeed, as was shown in an earlier chapter, all of the blessings associated with baptism are elsewhere and much more frequently associated with faith, and very insistently with faith alone.

Now the baptist believes that the only way to protect baptism itself from becoming a snare and a false means of support is to insist that the connection between baptism and faith is clear, recognizable, fundamental and unequivocal. He fears that this is not so in the case of an infant. To identify the faith involved as being that of the parents, the sponsors, the church or the hope that one day the infant will believe, is to him not sufficient. It puts a gap in time or condition between the act of baptism and the personal faith of the candidate. By doing so it focuses attention in the wrong place. The blessings associated in Scripture with faith-plus-baptism will in the case of paedobaptism unavoidably be associated with the baptism rather than the faith. However much is said about faith coming later, the process has started off on the wrong foot. Many people baptized in infancy will grow up unaware of the need to come to personal faith. The only safeguard, he believes, is to keep baptism until faith has been expressed.

g. The doctrine of baptism

Finally, there are to be considered the doctrinal statements about the meaning of baptism which are made in the New Testament (see chapter 1). Baptists insist that we must go much further than asking how the apostles practised baptism, and ask how they *explained* it. They admit that the absence of any specific mention of paedobaptism might conceivably be explained away, but what cannot be explained away, they insist, is the meaning given to baptism by the apostles. It is given a significance which can be applied only to believers. Forgiveness of sins, new birth, the gift of the Holy Spirit, identification with Christ in his death and resurrection, are all associated in many places with faith, and in some places with faith-expressed-in-baptism.

That this is all true of the believer is easy to understand, and that the believer expresses his confidence in its truth by being baptized is equally easy to understand. It might well be possible to go further (with some modern baptists) and agree that baptism may to the believer make it more subjectively true and more vividly experienced. But to say that it is true in any sense at all of an infant long before faith is expressed is really to say that an infant's baptism is fundamentally different from a believer's baptism. The two baptisms are really different sacraments. They make different requirements of the candidate, are differently related to the preaching of the gospel, and are differently connected to the blessing associated with them. Since it is believer's baptism that is described and explained in the New Testament, most baptists do not feel able to give the name baptism to a ceremony to which small children are brought. Again, it is not a matter of bigotry, but one of deep theological moment, and the baptist should be able to expect understanding, if not agreement.

Fundamentally, then, the baptist approach can well be summarized in the famous words of Spurgeon: 'If we could find (infant baptism) in the Word of God, we should adopt it. It would help us out of a great difficulty, for it would take away from us that reproach which is attached to us – that we are odd and do not as other people do. But we have looked well through the Bible and cannot find it, and do not believe it is there; nor do we believe that others can find infant baptism in the Scriptures, unless they themselves first put it there.'[1]

[1] Spurgeon, *Autobiography* (Banner of Truth, 1967), Vol. I, pp. 154–155.

Part II

Baptism & History

4
After the apostles

During the closing decade of the second century a brilliant young barrister was converted to Christ in the bustling North African city of Carthage. Of the circumstances surrounding his conversion we know little, but we do know that remarkably soon afterwards Quintus Septimius Florens Tertullianus (known to history as Tertullian) became one of the most outstanding Christians of his day and left in his writings a legacy which has influenced the church ever since. Because Tertullian was the first major Christian thinker to write in Latin, his theological terminology has become definitive in the Western church and its offshoots.

Addressing himself to the needs of the moment, Tertullian wrote fluently on a variety of subjects. First, he vigorously defended the Christian faith against the persecuting attacks of Roman governors. Then he produced theological, ethical and disciplinary treatises for Christians themselves much in the way the Apostle Paul had composed his letters to the sons and daughters of the infant church. And when 'a certain female viper from the Cainite sect . . . carried off a good number with her exceptionally pestilential doctrine, making a particular point of demolishing baptism',[1] Tertullian addressed himself to the subject and produced *De baptismo*, his *Homily on baptism*.

[1] Tertullian, *De baptismo*, I.5.

De baptismo is supremely important for the modern baptismal controversy because it contains the first explicit reference in all Christian writing, Scripture included, to the practice of paedobaptism, and significantly, it is a protest against it. Tertullian writes: 'It follows that deferment of baptism is more profitable, in accordance with each person's character and attitude, and even age: *and especially so as regards children*. For what need is there, if there really is no need, for even their sponsors to be brought into peril, seeing they may possibly themselves fail of their promises by death, or be deceived by the subsequent development of an evil disposition? It is true our Lord says, Forbid them not to come to me. So let them come, when they are growing up, when they are learning, when they are being taught what they are coming to: let them be made Christians when they have become competent to know Christ. *Why should innocent infancy come with haste* to the remission of sins? Shall we take less cautious action in this than we take in worldly matters? Shall one who is not trusted with earthly property be entrusted with heavenly? Let them first learn how to ask for salvation, so that you may be seen to have given to one that asketh. With no less reason ought the unmarried also to be delayed until they either marry or are firmly established in continence: until then, temptation lies in wait for them, for virgins because they are ripe for it, and for widows because of their wandering about. All who understand what a burden baptism is will have more fear of obtaining it than of its postponement. Faith unimpaired has no doubt of its salvation.'[1]

What is immediately apparent from this extract is that some of Tertullian's arguments possess a familiar ring, although others sound strange to modern ears. The real issue, however, surrounding this passage, with regard to infant baptism, lies in the question: Against what was Tertullian protesting? An old-established practice reaching

[1] Tertullian, *De baptismo*, XVIII.19–34. Italics ours.

back to the days of the apostles themselves? Or a new development taking place throughout the church at the turn of the second and third centuries? Among scholars the question has been as keenly debated as the wider issue about infant baptism itself. Of recent years the debate has been conducted at the highest level between Joachim Jeremias of the University of Göttingen[1] and Kurt Aland of the University of Münster.[2] Suffice to say, whatever the answer may be, within thirty years of the publication of *De baptismo* Hippolytus in the West and Origen in the East both regarded infant baptism as a normal practice, deriving its origin and authority from the apostles. Of equal significance is the fact that Tertullian's protest against paedobaptism was part of a wider protest against hasty baptism in general in which virgins and widows were particularly included. To ascertain the reasons for this protest it is necessary to enquire into the meaning of baptism as it was understood in the post-apostolic church.

Three descriptions of baptism during the first two centuries of the church's life are available to the modern student of Christian history. The first of these is found in the *Didache* or *Teaching of the twelve apostles*, a manual of uncertain date which none the less, according to the almost unanimous opinion of scholars, displays the character of a very primitive Christian community. Baptism is to be preceded by fasting and is to be administered in the threefold Name in running water. If running water or a pool is not available water may be poured on the head in which case a threefold affusion must accompany the recitation of the threefold Name.[3]

The second account of baptism comes in the *First Apology* of Justin Martyr written about the middle of the

[1] See Jeremias, *Infant baptism in the first four centuries* and *The origins of infant baptism* (SCM, 1963).
[2] See Aland, *Did the early church baptize infants?* (SCM, 1963).
[3] See *Didache*, VII.1–4.

second century. Justin was a philosopher who came to Christianity from dissatisfaction with the philosophies of his day. Having been converted, he presented the Roman authorities, in his *Apologies*, with a reasoned defence of Christianity. His efforts, however, were of little avail, for, as his name implies, he died as a martyr in Rome about AD 163 during the reign of the Emperor Marcus Aurelius.

Baptism, for Justin, is the means whereby men and women are dedicated to God and made new through Christ. It is given to as many as are persuaded and believe that the things are true which are taught by the church and undertake to be able to live accordingly. It is preceded by prayer and fasting by the candidates and congregation. Then they are brought where there is water and are born again, being washed in the Name of the Father, the Son and the Holy Spirit. Baptism is administered that the baptized may obtain remission of sins formerly committed. It is followed by prayers and the celebration of communion along with the assembled congregation.[1]

The third account is found in the *Apostolic tradition* of Hippolytus which is generally regarded as descriptive of the practice of the church in Rome at the turn of the second and third centuries. Here, baptism is much more elaborate than in the earlier accounts. It is preceded by anointing with the oil of exorcism and prayer for the departure of spirits. Threefold baptism by immersion is then accompanied by interrogation and affirmation of belief in the clauses of the Apostles' Creed. This is followed by further anointing with the oil of thanksgiving, the laying-on-of-hands by the bishop and prayers. Through baptism, remission of sins is obtained through the laver of regeneration of the Holy Spirit.[2]

To be rightly understood, these descriptions of baptism must be set against the phenomenal growth of the church

[1] See Justin, *First apology*, 61, 65.

[2] See Hippolytus, *Apostolic tradition*, 21, 22.

which was taking place by the end of the second century. By that time Christianity was fast becoming a very popular religion. It frequently came into conflict with the Roman authorities for that very reason. Its growing influence was regarded by successive emperors with suspicion and fear. Its voice was heard throughout Europe and the Near East. Large numbers were pressing into its ranks for a mixture of reasons: its social concern, its superior morality, its kindness to the slave, its words of certainty about the after-life.

Because the church was growing so rapidly by no means all of its converts had really turned from paganism. Periodic times of persecution thinned out the ranks of the half-converted but after the official 'recognition' of Christianity by the Emperor Constantine in AD 313 by the Edict of Milan the rate of rapid growth became an avalanche as thousands swelled the church's ranks. In these circumstances it is hardly surprising that the outward trappings of religion made more appeal than its deeper convictions. And since baptism was the means of entry into the church it is no less surprising that changes in the administration and understanding of baptism reflected the growing importance and position of Christianity.

When the three accounts of baptism cited above are compared with accounts of baptisms described in the New Testament, three areas of development are immediately apparent. First there was a development in the extent of baptismal preparation. Secondly, there was a development in the actual administration of the rite itself. Thirdly, there was a development in the understanding of the rite.

In the New Testament, as will be demonstrated in more detail in Part three, the baptism of adults was preceded by little or no preparation. Thus the Pentecostal converts were baptized on the same day as they heard the gospel (see Acts 2:41). The Philippian gaoler was baptized 'the same hour of the night' as he believed in the Lord

Jesus (Acts 16:33), and so on. In the post-apostolic church this was all changed. In the *Didache*, baptism was administered only when the candidates had 'first recited all these things,' that is, all things concerning the Way of Life and the Way of Death, the subject matter of the manual.[1] In Justin, baptism was given only to 'as many as are persuaded and believe that the things are true which are taught by us and said to be true, and undertake to be able to live accordingly,'[2] thus implying a period of instruction and probation beforehand. In Hippolytus, assent to the Apostles' Creed during baptism would not have been required without previous instruction in its meaning.

It was because the church grew so rapidly during the early centuries of its life that baptismal preparation became necessary. It represented an attempt by the leaders to limit those who would join the church for the wrong reasons. By Hippolytus's time (the period of the early church's most rapid growth) the system of baptismal preparation had become institutionalized into the 'catechumenate'. Catechumens were people anxious to enter the church but kept in a period of probation until they were considered to be ready for full membership. Regarded as Christians, they were permitted to attend all of the services, but not to take communion. They were required to attend instruction classes in which they received moral and religious teaching for as long as three years. At the end of their probationary period those who still wished it were received into full church membership, and at this point were baptized. The rest could remain as catechumens, in the outer circle of church activity. It was a thoughtful and impressive method of dealing with a difficult problem. To increase its effectiveness, the act of baptism was invested with a tremendous aura of solemnity and crisis. All of the long catechetical teaching pointed towards it. A theology

[1] *Didache*, VII.1.
[2] Justin, *First apology*, 61.

of baptism gave it immense significance. Every artifice of symbol and ceremony was used to make the baptismal service a memorable occasion.

The catechetical lectures of Cyril, bishop of Jerusalem in the fourth century, show clearly the development of this method to a peak of near-perfection. Carefully constructed, they covered every aspect of Christianity. The lessons themselves were punctuated by impressive symbolic acts, and each lesson began by the bishop breathing on the catechists, covering their heads, exorcising them and reading solemn scriptural warnings.

Having taken them through detailed instruction on Christian ethics and doctrine, the bishop eventually reached the baptismal lessons themselves. He warned his hearers that this was a secret which should not be shared with unbelievers. 'We are handing on to you a mystery, a hope of the Age to come. Guard the mystery from those who would waste this prize.'[1] He then referred to the sixth chapter of Romans and expounded its symbolism of death and resurrection with Christ. 'Christ is here in your midst,' he concluded dramatically. 'He is ready, O you who want to be baptized, to bring you by the Holy Spirit into the presence of the Father.'[2]

The baptismal service eventually took place at dawn on Easter Sunday, in the flooring of the sepulchre, believed to be the very site of Christ's tomb. No effort was spared to make the ceremony deeply impressive with its flaming torches, chanting voices, white-robed candidates, solemn questions, ceremonies of exorcism, anointing, laying-on-of-hands and the threefold immersion of perhaps several hundred converts.

Cyril's baptismal service brings us to the second important development in early church baptism when compared with the New Testament, the actual administration of the

[1] *Catechetical lectures of Cyril of Jerusalem*, 9.
[2] *Ibid.*, 14.

rite. In the New Testament and in the *Didache*, baptism was a simple affair involving little more than immersion or affusion in the Name of Jesus or perhaps of the Trinity. By the time of Cyril, and indeed by the time of Hippolytus, all this has changed. To the actual washing of baptism has been added exorcism, anointing and the episcopal laying-on-of-hands, quite apart from embellishments surrounding the baptismal act itself. When this change is linked with the understanding given to baptism in the fourth century it is easy to see how quickly thereafter the church came to hold the erroneous views of the rite particularly associated with the Middle Ages.

While there is ample evidence that the early Fathers understood the whole scriptural doctrine of baptism, it is also evident that most of them stressed the connection between baptism and the forgiveness of sins more than anything else. Thus Justin could say that baptism was administered that 'we . . . may obtain the remission of sins formerly committed'.[1] Hippolytus tells us that the baptized were made 'worthy to obtain remission of sins through the laver of regeneration of the Holy Spirit'.[2] Other examples from many other early writers could be multiplied.

The modern Christian is justified in asking if the early Fathers considered that forgiveness was automatically bestowed in baptism without repentance and faith being necessary on the part of the baptized. In some of their statements they sometimes spoke *as if* this were so (in much the same way as some modern evangelists speak *as if* walking to the front at the end of a meeting makes a man a Christian) but on balance the evidence points against this conclusion. Baptism was important precisely because it was a visible sign (*sign*, not means) of an invisible reality already taking place. The new convert (it was assumed) really regretted his past, really trusted in Christ, really

[1] Justin, *First apology*, 61.

[2] Hippolytus, *Apostolic tradition*, 22.

embraced the promises of God and really wished to live a new life; for those reasons he came to baptism as the visible mark of coming to Christ. But if the leaders resisted an automatic connection between baptism and forgiveness there is less certainty that the many 'converts' of the second, third and fourth centuries shared their reservations, and this, with all its implications, brings us back to Tertullian.

If baptism secured the forgiveness of sins (and increasingly in the popular mind, if not the educated mind, it did so) what of sins committed after baptism? Was there any forgiveness for these? Initially, the answer was, No, although later the appalling implications of this conclusion forced theologians to distinguish between sins for which there was forgiveness (called later still venial sins) and sins for which there was no forgiveness (mortal sins). Tertullian himself followed this line of thinking, listing the 'deadly sins' of idolatry, blasphemy, murder, adultery, fornication, false witness and fraud for which there was no forgiveness if they were committed after baptism.[1]

If post-baptismal sin were unforgivable, might it not be better to delay baptism, even to the point of death, in order to avoid apostasy and to die in the certainty of forgiveness? To many Christians, particularly during the fourth century when thousands were flocking into the church after the official recognition of Christianity, this was a particularly attractive solution to the problem of post-baptismal sin. While the reasoning is not carried to this conclusion by Tertullian its beginnings are clearly to be found in his thought. '*Deferment of baptism* is more profitable, in accordance with each person's character and attitude. . . . With no less reason ought the unmarried also to be delayed until they either marry or are firmly established in continence: until then, *temptation lies in wait for* them. . . . All who understand *what a burden baptism is* will

[1] Tertullian, *De pudicitia*.

have more fear of obtaining it than of its postponement.'[1] For the same reason children should not be baptized lest their sponsors be found to have made promises for those in whom 'an evil disposition'[2] subsequently develops.

Once baptism was given to children, of course, a further problem arose. If baptism secured the remission of sins, for what sins did new-born children need to be forgiven? The answer here lay in the development of the doctrine of original sin, although, as has been earlier shown, this doctrine grew out of paedobaptism rather than the other way round.[3] If, of course, a new-born baby does need forgiveness from birth, and if forgiveness is secured by baptism, then it is imperative that the infant be baptized. And whatever the ultimate position on paedobaptism may be there can be little doubt that belief in the infant's need for forgiveness provided the main impetus for the growth of paedobaptism from the second century onwards. And it is on this score that Tertullian had his most serious doubts. 'Why should innocent infancy', he asks, 'come with haste to the remission of sins?'[4]

For a while his protest was heeded. The movement in favour of delaying baptism gained ground. But during the fifth century the towering figure of Augustine of Hippo with his powerful reassertion of the doctrine of original guilt settled the issue for a thousand years. Paedobaptism became the norm, and as by then the great expansion of the church among adults had run its course, adult baptism became increasingly rare and almost unknown. With the decline of adult baptism went, too, the decline of the catechumenate, as instruction before baptism was replaced, of necessity, with instruction after baptism. Yet that instruction became increasingly strange to modern ears.

[1] Tertullian, *De baptismo*, XVIII.
[2] *Ibid.*
[3] See above, p. 38.
[4] Tertullian, *De baptismo*, XVIII.

For although baptized infants grew up believing that their baptism had brought them forgiveness, eternal life, membership of the church and entry into the family of God, their position in that family became increasingly insecure. In time a vast system of priests, penances and pilgrimages was needed to preserve their spiritual lives, while even after the intercession of saints, the assistance of Mary, the prayers of the church and the indulgences of the pope, centuries in purgatory still awaited them after death before their souls were cleansed from sin and prepared for heaven.

Whether or not Tertullian was right in his protest against paedobaptism, the modern Christian must judge for himself. Of one thing, however, he can be certain. When the specific reasoning of the late second century is stripped from Tertullian's thought, the lines of the modern baptismal controversy can be found in his protest. Should baptism be a conscious or an unconscious experience? Let children come to baptism, says Tertullian, 'when they are growing up, when they are learning, when they are being taught what they are coming to'.[1] Should baptism reflect a man's personal accountability to God in the matter of his salvation, or may it be given him by others? Let children be made Christians, says Tertullian, 'when they have become competent to know Christ'.[2] In the final analysis, is it baptism in water or faith in Christ which saves? And might not baptism in infancy become a hindrance to faith in maturity? 'Faith unimpaired' by baptism (!), declares Tertullian, 'has no doubt of its salvation.'[3]

Two other developments in baptism in the post-apostolic period need to be noted, for their effects are still with us today. The first of these concerned the rite of confirmation, the second the doctrine of Christian sacralism.

[1] Tertullian, *De baptismo*, XVIII.
[2] *Ibid.*, XVIII.
[3] *Ibid.*

Confirmation

As has been shown, entry into the church, in the *Didache* as in the New Testament, was a simple affair involving washing in water in the Name of the Father, the Son and the Holy Spirit. By the end of the second century it had become much more complex, involving exorcism, anointing and the laying-on-of-hands as well as the actual baptism. Essential to the ceremony was the presence of the bishop.

Once paedobaptism became widespread, however, during and after the fifth century, it frequently became physically impossible for the bishop to preside at all baptisms. Yet because paedobaptism was believed to be imperative, and because many infants died shortly after their birth, the complex initiation rite which was universally called baptism had to be split up. At birth, or as soon as possible thereafter, the infant received the baptism-in-water part of the baptismal ceremony, while the other parts of the ceremony (anointing, laying-on-of-hands, *etc.*) were given later when the bishop came on his rounds and visited the parish. There is ample evidence to show, however, that the medieval church none the less regarded baptism in water and laying-on-of-hands as one rite of initiation whereby entrance was gained into the church.

At the time of the Reformation, Calvin and others of the leading Reformers appear to have misunderstood the purpose of the episcopal visitations, regarding them as times when those baptized in infancy 'confirmed' their baptismal vows and so were fully admitted into the church. Thus began the Protestant rite of confirmation. With the Reformers' emphasis on faith it became a suitable moment for those baptized as infants, now responsibly mature, to express their personal faith in Christ. But problems were to arise. Was confirmation scriptural, and if so, what was its significance? These and related problems will be discussed in greater detail later on. Suffice to say, since the Reformation confirmation has been a practice seeking a theology and this to the frequent embarrassment of Protestant Christians.

Christian sacralism

Sacralism is the view that all the members of a particular nation should be bound together by loyalty to the same religion, which same religion gives political authority to the leaders of that nation. Religious dissent thus becomes the same as political subversion. Christian sacralism developed as Christianity became the official religion of the Roman Empire during and after the fourth century. Its importance will be explained in greater detail later when it had a significant effect on baptismal developments at the time of the Reformation. It was so taken for granted by early Christian missionaries that they regarded the conversion of heathen rulers as amounting to the conversion of all their people and to their automatic incorporation within Christendom. Like confirmation it survived the Reformation, continuing to be embodied in the legal relationships between church and state which were laid down, at that time, in Protestant Europe. It naturally leads to paedobaptism, for it regards birth into the nation as amounting to entry into the church. Where the view is still held it naturally continues to pose a major stumbling-block in the way of reconciliation between paedobaptist and baptists.

By the end of the fifth century the lines of modern paedobaptismal practice were drawn. Yet, contrary to much modern understanding, they were not as universally applied before the Reformation as is commonly believed. The system had its critics who sometimes maintained a contrary position in the teeth of bitter opposition, fanatical persecution and even death. To those who so suffered we must now turn.

5
Medieval underground

In the year 1530 a fascinating meeting took place in a Piedmont valley between two great Christian movements. Leaders of the strange and mysterious Waldensians, called 'barbes', met ministers of the new Reformed churches of Geneva. The *barbes* brought a Christianity which stretched back no-one knew how long: some said to apostolic times. The ministers were the vanguard of a sweeping new movement which would soon represent Christ in every continent. They found that their views differed on many points. But heartily did they agree on two issues. The Catholic Church had forfeited any right to be regarded as the voice of Christianity. And God was at work in both of their movements, drawing men to read the Bible, believe the gospel, turn to Christ and live new lives as children of God. Each group went home rejoicing, spreading the good news that the gospel had more witnesses in the past and the present than anyone had suspected. The Reformation had come into contact with the medieval underground.

This useful term covers a multitude of movements, sects and heresies which, throughout the whole of the Middle Ages, gave very varied expression to a widespread and indestructible current of opposition to the Catholic Church. There was a time when the only sources of information about the heretics were the calumnies of their accusers and persecutors. Now there is a wealth of information available in the records of what they said in their own defence when on trial, and what they taught before they were arrested. What emerges from these is a very different picture of the Middle Ages from the one which both Catholics and Protestants have tended to imagine.

True enough, the Catholic Church had the ear of Europe's leaders and the power of a massive organization. 'It is difficult for us today to imagine the immensity of that power in the Middle Ages . . . the Church controlled the sacraments, and the sacraments were essential to salvation. . . . With these prerogatives in his hand, and the Church at his back, the priest was omnipotent.'[1] But there was always a nagging voice of protest and doubt about this power. The voice was called heresy. Whenever possible it was ignored. If it could not be ignored its spokesmen were given some concessions and assimilated into the structure; if they could not be assimilated, they were maligned, accused, destroyed. Its secret meetings were broken up. A hundred different nicknames were given to its organizations. To a faithful Catholic who troubled to look into the situation continent-wide, heresy must have seemed a hydra-headed monster or a babel of discordant and contradictory beliefs. Yet a closer look revealed an odd sameness in the accusations brought against the heretics.

The Waldensians themselves are an example. Also called Vaudois, Poor Men of Lyons, Vallenses or simply Brethren, their permanent home seems to have been in the high valleys of Switzerland. They were certainly there in the eleventh century, and were still there five hundred years later when the Reformation had begun. But who and what were they? Dissident Catholics enjoying immunity from hostile attention in their remote valleys? Followers of Claudius, Bishop of Turin in the ninth century? Followers of Peter Waldo of Lyons in the twelfth century? What are

[1] Robinson, *Baptist principles* (Carey Kingsgate Press, 1935), p. 46.

we to make of the staggering assertion of the Dean of Notre Dame in Arras in the fourteenth century that one-third of Christendom sometimes attended their meetings and was Waldensian at heart?[1] What are we to make of the even more staggering claim they made to the Protestant Reformers that their line of descent could be traced back to the apostles themselves? How could an obscure group of protesters in Switzerland be responsible for a heresy taught everywhere between the Baltic and the Mediterranean? Was the word Waldensian in fact just a convenient label for any dissenting sect? Probably so. 'In 1184 Waldensianism began its long history as a sectarian movement, spreading throughout central Europe and absorbing in different regions the local heresies in ever new combinations.'[2] It would be a gross over-simplification to regard medieval heresy as one distinguishable and uniform movement. Protestants have sometimes been tempted to do so. In reply to the Catholic boast of one unchanging church in every century, periodic Protestant attempts have been made to trace a 'thin red line' of evangelical witness through every century too. The attempt has provided modern Christians with some embarrassing bed-fellows whose only common factor was a dislike of Rome and all her ways. 'Dissent' and 'protest' would perhaps be more accurate titles of the medieval underground than either 'evangelicalism' or 'heresy'.[3] Some of the movements were in fact heretical. All were deeply medieval. Some could fairly be called evangelical.

Certainly some themes constantly reappear in the heresy trials. Protest groups condemned the 'worldliness' of the

[1] Verduin, *The reformers and their stepchildren* (Paternoster Press, 1964), p.173.

[2] Williams, *The radical reformation* (Weidenfeld & Nicolson, 1962), p. 520.

[3] As *e.g.* in Burton, *Dissent and reform in the early Middle Ages* (Cambridge University Press, 1968).

official church, rejected its priestly system, regarded its sacraments with suspicion and sought a biblical simplicity of religious life. But of course all of these issues raised problems with the sacrament of baptism, which was administered to infants for the washing away of original sin where the church was in power, and administered *en masse* to whole regions on the borders of Christendom when some local king or ruler embraced the Catholic faith. Searching questions were asked. If the church is hopelessly corrupt, what of the validity of its baptisms? If priestcraft and sacramentalism are to be rejected, should baptism be rejected too? Is a call to personal commitment consistent with a baptism indiscriminately applied? Various answers were given, for many disconnected 'heresies' were involved, but generally speaking, 'Salvation by believing response to the preached Word and salvation by sacramental manipulation, lay in mortal combat with each other all through medieval times.'[1]

The Waldenses or Waldensians are the only medieval sect which modern Protestants unequivocally recognize as holding the same faith as themselves. When, as we have seen, Swiss Reformers met Waldensian leaders, there was mutual delight. 'The Waldensians provided the early Protestants with a splendid riposte to the question, "Where was your church before Luther?" '[2]

Caught up in the Reformation, the Waldensians evolved from a rather amorphous 'movement' into a modern 'church' which is the strongest Protestant denomination in Italy to this day. Nowadays their claims to antiquity are modest. They trace their undoubted history back to the eleventh century, and speak in general terms of links with earlier movements. Their career in the Middle Ages was a chequered one. At times they were content to be a ginger

[1] Verduin, *The reformers and their stepchildren*, p. 153.

[2] *The new international dictionary of the Christian church* (Paternoster Press, 1974), p. 1026.

group within Catholicism, working hopefully for reform, and for the sake of safety accepting Catholic sacraments with a secret mental reservation. It was a practice which Calvin was later to scorn as 'Nicodemism', but that was a little unfair. The attitude arose not from cowardice, but from a deeply 'inward and spiritual' view of worship and faith. Rightly or wrongly, they simply dismissed enforced visible sacraments as an unwelcome but irrelevant fact of life which did the soul neither good nor harm.[1] At other times they adopted an almost monastic policy, and indeed Peter Waldo, their first undisputed leader, bore a strong resemblance to Francis of Assisi (whom he preceded by thirty years). The hesitant papal approval given to the Franciscans was only just denied to the 'Poor Men of Lyons' whom Peter Waldo led. Yet at other times they were a much more recognizably evangelistic movement, and more than once before and after the Reformation experienced what can only be described as an evangelical awakening.

Not surprisingly, then, their attitude to baptism was not always the same. One scholar maintains, 'Infant Baptism was widely regarded as desirable for salvation,'[2] while another asserts, 'The Baptism of believers by immersion was common to the Waldenses.'[3]

The truth seems to be that they practised paedobaptism quite widely among their own children. In the remote Alpine valleys where the movement always survived whatever its fortunes elsewhere, whole communities were Waldensian, and it was virtually certain that children born among them would maintain the faith in adult life. But when Catholics were converted to their movement, they 'rebaptized' them, for they were conceived as turning from the false church to the true. This seems to indicate that

[1] See Williams, *The radical reformation*, p. 578, for a full discussion.
[2] *Ibid.*, p. 526.
[3] Broadbent, *The pilgrim church* (Pickering & Inglis, 1935), p. 130.

they were opposed to *Catholic* baptism rather than to *infant* baptism. It was an attitude which was later to irritate Martin Luther when he came across it – especially when they cheerfully applied the same policy to Lutherans!

'They baptize little ones . . . and rebaptize those who come to them from us.'[1] 'What the Waldensians had against "christening" was not the infancy of the recipient, but the Constantinian overtones of the ritual. Therefore they rebaptized converts from the prevailing Church and practised infant baptism in the case of their own little ones.'[2]

Here, then, is a notable example of a respectable 'Protestant' movement with a dual approach to baptism, whose followers were able to live charitably together despite differences in baptismal practice.

In contrast to the Waldensians are the Paulicians. They survived and sometimes flourished on the Eastern borders of Europe, and had a similar relationship with the Orthodox Church to that of Waldensianism with Rome. Their stance was one of more open opposition, and they aroused corresponding anger. They endured merciless persecution, and sometimes responded by taking up arms. With cheerful impartiality these were accused of being Manichaeans and Muhammadans, and it is not easy to decide just what they were in fact. Clearly the worst accusations were quite unjustified, and as with all investigation into the beliefs of the medieval underground, it must be assumed that those who did not scruple to murder them would not hesitate to malign them.

Their origins went far back beyond the Middle Ages – certainly as far as the sixth century in Asia Minor. They insistently maintained that they represented not a heresy, not even a reform movement, but a primitive form of Christianity which had resisted the innovations of Orthodoxy. As late as 1828, a colony of their survivors settled

[1] Verduin, *The reformers and their stepchildren*, p. 196. [2] *Ibid.*

in Armenia and brought an ancient manual of doctrine, allegedly dating back for a thousand years. It was translated into English seventy years later as *The key of truth* and created a sensation. They were hailed as 'Ancient Oriental Baptists . . . in many respects Protestants before Protestantism'.[1]

Later scholars were inclined to be a little less enthusiastic, especially about the Paulician doctrine of Christ, and a modern dictionary describes them more cautiously as 'an evangelical antihierarchical sect originating in the seventh century . . . whose characteristic doctrines include Adoptionist Christology, the Authority of Scripture . . . and Believers' Baptism'.[2] 'There are three divine mysteries which God proclaimed,' wrote the author of *The key of truth*. 'First, repentance; second, baptism; third, holy communion. These three He gave to the adults and not to catechumens who have not repented or are unbelieving.'[3]

The Paulician convert, or the Paulician child grown to maturity, was baptized in a kneeling position in the water of any convenient river. He confessed his past sin and present faith 'with love and tears' as he knelt in the water . . . 'and then as he that has believed completes his holy profession of faith, the elect one (*i.e.* the minister) instantly takes the water into his hands, and looking up to heaven . . . shall empty out the water over the head, saying: In the Name of Father and Son and Holy Spirit is baptized this man or woman, by the testimony of the congregation here present.'[4]

The Paulician approach to Orthodox Christianity was one of radical protest. They regarded the use of icons and

[1] Adeney, *The Greek and eastern churches*. Quoted in Robinson, *Baptist principles*, p. 58.

[2] *The new international dictionary of the Christian church*, p. 755.

[3] *The key of truth*, p. 116 f. Quoted in Robinson, *Baptist principles*, p. 59.

[4] *Ibid.*, p. 96. Quoted in *Baptist principles*, p. 60.

holy pictures and the dependence on priests and sacraments as the invasion of Christianity by pagan customs. Significantly they maintained that one of the principal causes of this invasion was precisely the enforced baptism of still semi-pagan adults and the baptism of infants incapable of faith. Non-christian habits and thought-forms, they maintained, were thus bound to creep into the churches. There can be little doubt that the Paulicians taught Adoptionism, that most persistent and attractive of Christological heresies from which few Christian movements have been completely immune.[1] This lessens the value of their witness in some respects, but does not diminish the interest and importance of their approach to baptism. We can read of their objections to baptizing 'the unbelieving, the reasonless, and the unrepentant'. It must be remembered that at that early stage the indiscriminate, and even enforced, baptism of adult pagans was commonplace on the frontiers of Christendom. However, any form of paedobaptism was banned by them. For the children of Paulician believers there was prescribed a moving service of thanksgiving, parental vows, naming and prayerful dedication. Baptism itself was administered only to those who 'earnestly sought' it – another indication that believers' baptism, not merely adult baptism, was in mind. Many Paulicians preferred to delay baptism until the age of thirty, so as more closely to resemble Christ. They linked the descent of the Holy Spirit upon Jesus at Jordan with his own awareness of his unique relationship with the Father, and with the Christian's awareness of adoption into the family of God. It was this emphasis that led them on to thin ice in their Christology – a fact which the Orthodox were quick to grasp and to exploit.

The medieval underground was a complex phenomenon, and must be approached with caution in support of an

[1] Adoptionism is the view that Jesus was a man of blameless life who became the adoptive Son of God.

argument. Yet we shall see its successor during and after the Reformation, and hear far-off echoes of its voice in modern movements. From the point of view of this book it underlines one point: that a man's attitude towards Christendom in general and baptism in particular will be shaped by the state of religion as he finds it. In their situation, the medieval 'heretics' tended to see paedo-baptism as a representative sacrament of superstition and worldly religion. In contrast, adult baptism came to represent salvation by faith, protest against corrupt Christendom, and suffering for the sake of purified religion.

The situation today may be very different, but the questions they posed and only partially answered, are still with us.

6
Reformation tragedy

On a bitterly cold January day in 1527 a boat on the River Limmat was carrying a man to his death. At his trial Felix Manz had freely confessed to being a teacher of doctrines forbidden in Switzerland. 'We bring together those who are willing to accept Christ, obey the Word, and follow in His footsteps. We unite them by baptism, and leave the rest in their present conviction.'[1] Pressed to enlarge on his views about baptism in particular, he admitted: 'More is involved in Baptism: things on which I prefer not to enlarge just now.'[2] The Clerk of Courts wrote an explanatory comment in the records: 'They do not allow Infant Baptism. In this way they will put an end to secular authority.'[3]

It seems an extraordinary comment. More extraordinary still is the outburst of his accuser Ulrich Zwingli, Switzerland's heroic Protestant Reformer. Speaking of men like this he cried, 'Let him who talks about going under (the water) go under.'[4]

[1] Verduin, *The reformers and their stepchildren*, p. 74.

[2] *Quellen zur Geschichte der Taufer in der Schweiz*, p. 51. (A German collection of original sources of Reformation material, hereafter called *Quellen*.)

[3] Verduin, *The reformers and their stepchildren*, p. 205.

[4] *Ibid.*, p. 217. The books by Verduin and Williams have brought a mass of documentation to the attention of British readers, and have led

To the authorities it seemed poetic justice. Felix Manz was condemned to death by drowning.

Led into the boat, he was forced to sit up and his arms were passed around his bent knees and bound at the wrists. Next a stick was pushed between knees and elbows to secure him in this position. The boat was rowed to the centre of the river, and the helpless prisoner was thrown overboard, to choke in the dark deep waters.

Protestant had killed Protestant for the crime of obeying God's Word as he understood it.

How could so strange a thing happen, just ten years after the beginning of the Reformation in Europe? It happened because the Reformation of the sixteenth century rediscovered the New Testament gospel, but failed to recreate the New Testament church.

To say this is not to belittle the achievement of the great Reformers: Luther, Zwingli, Calvin and their colleagues. What they did was astonishing. The world was permanently changed by their endeavour. The Christian gospel, buried under a mountain of priestcraft and superstition, was unearthed and revealed again as the good news of the free grace of God, offered directly to men in Jesus Christ. Taught by the rediscovered Scriptures, interpreted by the Holy Spirit, and worked out agonizingly in their own experience, this gospel first transformed the Reformers themselves. It gave them the courage to withstand powerful adversaries, the clarity to dismiss centuries of tradition and the conviction which enabled them to win the attention of multitudes. To acknowledge this is only just. But to deny that their efforts contained an element of error and confusion is to deny that they were human at all.

The facts are plain. The Reformers found the gospel and

---

to a drastic reconsideration of the Anabaptist movement by modern Christians. Williams's work is more detailed and comprehensive, but we have usually quoted Verduin, who writes in a simpler and more popular style.

preached it with immense effect to the conversion of many. In doing so, they destroyed the framework of medieval Christendom. But when they were required to replace that framework and to cater for those converts, they faltered and became confused and divided. The division of Protestantism into Lutheran, Calvinistic and Anglican forms shows this. The later subdivision of Calvinism into Presbyterian, Independent and Baptist denominations underlines it further. But the most convincing evidence is provided by the story of the tragic conflict which developed between the main-line Protestants and the Anabaptists. In that conflict the issue of baptism was raised, sometimes came close to being resolved, but eventually drove two parties into irreconcilable collision. As a result, the progress of the Reformation ground to a halt for a generation. As a further result, it has been argued, Protestantism lost the working-classes of Europe.

The Anabaptists of the sixteenth century present us with perplexing problems. The word means 're-baptizers'. Its use pin-points the two features held in common by a large number of separate radical movements. They all condemned the Reformation as half-hearted and incomplete. They all rejected paedobaptism, and baptized or rebaptized only those who came to a decisive experience of religious commitment. The same two things could be said of twentieth-century Pentecostals, Baptists, Brethren, Christadelphians, Mormons and Jehovah's Witnesses. To class all of these, orthodox and heretical, under the name Baptist is about as accurate and fair as to class all the sixteenth-century radicals together as Anabaptists. Political revolutionaries and anti-trinitarian mystics were lumped together in popular thinking with simple evangelical believers who wished to take the Reformation to what they believed to be its scriptural and logical conclusion. Some of them were converts of the Reformers. Others were survivors from the persecuted but persistent 'medieval underground'.

Today the Anabaptists are known by various names (the Reformation Radicals, the Second Front, the Reformers' Stepchildren, the Common Man's Reformers, *etc.*), and their moving story is only being revealed and understood as scholars unearth and interpret what they wrote about themselves, rather than what was often unjustly written about them. Once regarded with embarrassment as fanatics from the lunatic fringe of Christendom, they are now increasingly recognized as part of a movement which had genuine Christian strands, and whose witness carries a challenge for our day. The British writer who has most painstakingly collected and analysed their writings says, 'Christians of many denominations are finding themselves . . . closer to the despised sectaries of the Reformation Era than to the classical defenders of a reformed *corpus christianum*.'[1]

Basically, the Anabaptists were asking for a regenerate church membership. For a thousand years, they said, state and church had been in an alliance foreign to the nature of the gospel. As part of that alliance, baptism had become 'christening' – the artificial christianizing of a whole population. But now that the true nature of the gospel had been rediscovered, it was possible to break the false structure and return to the New Testament pattern – believers gathered together in a voluntary association, whose government and sacraments were no concern of the political power.

This is now generally acknowledged to be the basic tenet of the most Christian of the Anabaptist groups. As the church historian Latourette says, Anabaptism was 'a manifestation of a continuing strain in Christianity which had been present from the very beginning, and which, before and since the Reformation, has expressed itself in many forms'.[2]

[1] Williams, *The radical reformation*, p. 31.

[2] Latourette, *A history of Christianity* (Eyre & Spottiswoode, 1954; see bibliography for new edn.), p. 786.

It is interesting to see how baptism became the visible and verbal centre of the controversy. But, as so often before and since, the visible rite of baptism only focused a deeper and wider debate. This is the tragic significance of the story.

There was much in the teaching of the Radicals which followed logically enough from Martin Luther's own teaching, and in the early years he was very much attracted to them.

In his own groping for the light, he had found in himself only the depths of sin, in God only an inexorable justice, and in the church only a paraphernalia of sacraments and sacerdotalism which gave him no peace with God. Through studying the Bible with desperate intensity, he had come gradually to understand that 'the righteousness of God' means, not God's anger at sin, but his willingness out of sheer love to declare the sinner pardoned, acquitted, justified. To achieve this, the Father had delivered up his Son to suffer the consequences of men's sin. By his Spirit he now brings the sinner to repentance, faith, pardon, acceptance and sonship. What no amount of religious observance or moral effort could achieve, bccame freely available to the man who abandoned himself in faith to the Christ preached in the gospel.

This was Luther's great discovery. It might very well have led him to the conclusion that only those who thus believe and find assurance belong to the church, and that they should meet together as believers on the ground of that assurance. He nearly came to that position. In 1523, before the Anabaptists had emerged, and when the first stage of the Reformation was in full swing, he said, 'My intention is, in days to come, not to admit any when communion is held, save such as have been interviewed and have given suitable answers as to their personal faith. The rest would be excluded.'[1]

[1] In a letter to his friend Nicholas Haussman. Quoted in Verduin, *The reformers and their stepchildren*, p. 127.

But this was very much a vision for some possible future date. For Luther must not be thought of as a master-planner with every move anticipated and with a clear view of his goal. He was simply caught up in tremendous events and continually had to improvise. In 1517 when his voice first sounded in protest and the world woke up to his presence, he had no thoughts of destroying the Catholic Church. It was the only church he knew. Within its fold he had eventually discovered the gospel. Within its organization he had preached that gospel for two years. He wished only to draw the church's attention to the implications of that gospel on abuses which were sullying its life. And in 1517 one of the most flagrant abuses made him speak out – the selling of 'indulgences' for cash: the promise of so many years' remission from purgatory for the man who paid up, or for his deceased relatives: the solemn assurance that as the coin chinked in the box, the soul sprang from the flames.

From then onwards he gradually realized how deep and bitter the conflict was to be. In 1516 he was simply rejoicing in an experience of God's forgiveness. In 1517 he wished to apply his experience to the abuse of indulgences. In 1518 he believed the Pope to be mistaken, but hoped to enlighten him. By 1519 he believed that general councils of the historic church could be in grave error. By 1520 he concluded that the papacy was the great beast of the Apocalypse, due to be destroyed by the wrath of God.

But by that time, he was reorganizing Catholic parish churches wherever his influence was felt, so that gradually the shape of a 'Lutheran church' appeared. Here a liturgy would be changed; there an emphasis would be altered; in another place a superstition was quietly buried. The framework was there, and Luther and his colleagues worked away at its adaptation to more evangelical principles as they were hammered out on the anvil of experience and controversy. But the framework *was* there: a framework of state-supported churches, established by law in areas where all were considered to be Christians in some sense, and where the life of the church was one side of the life of the state. In fact two different things were happening, and the two would eventually collide. The Reformation had a popular following of ordinary folk who were enlightened and enthused by evangelical preaching, plus members of the old persecuted sects who found a national leader suddenly saying more or less what they had always believed. At the same time it had the support of authority: local princes who, for a mixture of religious, political and personal motives supported Luther's quarrel with Rome, and permitted him to influence the churches which came under their control.

What course, then, was Luther to follow? The increasingly belligerent answer of the enthusiasts was 'Scrap everything and start again. Leave the churches. Preach the gospel, baptize the converts, and gather them together for fellowship, breaking of bread and prayers.' The increasing pressure of events said, 'Tread carefully. A false move, and you lose the ear of Europe and find yourself leader of just another persecuted sect. Keep the framework and deal patiently and graciously with the people within it. Gradually remove abuses when people are ready to be rid of them. Recapture Christendom for Christ: parish churches, priests, princes and all.' But to abandon paedobaptism meant to abandon the whole church structure as it then was. How can you reform an organization and at the same time knock away its foundations?

'Consider what disruption would ensue if there should develop among us two categories, the baptized and the unbaptized,' said Luther's friend, Melanchthon. 'If baptism were to be discontinued for most people, an openly pagan way of life would come about.'[1] That was precisely the problem. The baptism of only consciously committed

[1] Melanchthon, *Works*, Vol. 20.

Christians seemed incompatible with the rebuilding of a reformed Christendom and the establishing of Christian nations. 'Precisely so,' said the enthusiasts. 'But who cares about rebuilding Christendom? The idea is a delusion anyway. Neither the word nor the idea is to be found in the New Testament. The sooner it is forgotten the better. Uncommitted people *are* pagans, whether they live in Germany or in China. Then why not say so?'

This was the real baptismal controversy. Both the fascination and the tragedy of the Reformation from this point arises from the fact that the problem was not resolved, and that equally earnest Christians moved gradually from two positions very close together, to two positions hopelessly opposed. Brothers in Christ who began by discussing together over their Bibles, literally finished by killing each other.

The sad story can perhaps be followed more clearly at Zurich than at Wittenberg.

The proudly independent Swiss with their self-ruling cities and powerful city councils found their own way into a reformed Christianity. In 1518 a young Catholic clergyman called Ulrich Zwingli was appointed 'people's priest' or 'common preacher' to the great cathedral at Zurich. He had just come through a period of spiritual struggle to a personal faith in Christ. In his very first sermon he announced to the startled congregation: 'It is to Christ I wish to lead you. He is the source of salvation. His Gospel is the power of God to all that believe.'[1] His powerful and popular preaching, which took the form of vivid expositions of Scripture, forcefully applied, gave the impression that 'a man from the apostolic age was standing before you'.[2]

In the next five years reforms were gradually introduced in Zurich, and then in other Swiss cities by what became

[1] D. W. Marshall, 'Approaches to the reformation of the church', *Evangelical Magazine* (special report), December 1965.

[2] *Quellen*, 6, p. 184.

the characteristically Zwinglian method: first evangelistic preaching, then a public debate arranged by the city council, finally a reform adopted and decreed by the council. In five years the churches were distinctively 'Protestant' with an evangelicalism more simple and more radical than that of the Lutheran churches. With the enthusiastic support of growing numbers of clergy, laity and city councillors, images were removed, the mass abolished, clergy permitted to marry and relics banished. By 1525 the churches of Switzerland had unequivocally broken with Rome.

At that very time the Anabaptist controversy developed. Zwingli had given baptism much thought. 'Nothing grieves me more than that *at present* I must baptize children, for I know it ought not to be done.'[1] But his position was difficult. His office in the cathedral, which he employed with devastating effect, was held by arrangement with the civic authorities. Slowly but surely (more surely than the church authorities!) they were defending his action, accepting his reforms and giving effect to them. 'But if I were to stop the practice of Infant Baptism, I would lose my office.'[2]

To call this cowardice would be unjust. With fearless courage he defied every convention and every authority when once he became convinced that a reform was necessary for the sake of the gospel. He did not consider this to be such a case. 'I leave baptism untouched. I call it neither right nor wrong. If we were to baptize as Christ instituted it, then we would not baptize any person until he reached the years of discretion, for I find Infant Baptism nowhere written or practised. But we must practise it now so as not to offend our fellow men. . . . It is better not to preach (adult baptism) until the world is ready to receive it.'[3]

[1] Verduin, *The reformers and their stepchildren*, p. 198.
[2] *Ibid.*, p. 199.
[3] *Quellen*, 9, p. 186.

Unfortunately, while the world was still unready to receive it, there were men in the church eager to practise it! Conrad Grebel was one of Zwingli's converts. By 1523 he was chafing at the slowness of his leadership in reform. By 1524 he had come to his own conclusion about baptism and church membership in general, and rejecting paedo-baptism was gathering an informal group of converted and enthusiastic people for worship and teaching. Known popularly as 'Swiss Brethren', they became a church-within-the-church, and then a separate movement. Both Zwingli and the civil authorities were embarrassed by them, and in January 1525 the city council ordered them to disband their movement and particularly to desist from 'rebaptizing'. Grebel refused to do so, and after an evangelistic trip around Switzerland in which he won many converts, he was imprisoned, escaped and died in hiding two years later.

By this time another leader had appeared. Balthasar Hubmaier, a Catholic priest and an opponent of Luther, had a dramatic conversion. The two influences which led to this were Lutheranism and the teaching of the 'Bohemian Brethren', survivors of the 'medieval underground'. The latter taught baptism for believers only and (unusually for that time) by immersion. Hubmaier came to accept this position, and after thoroughly evangelizing his own parish in Waldshut, he baptized three hundred members of his parish church. Shortly after, the tide of war lapped over that region, and he fled into Switzerland and settled in Zurich. Having just silenced one troublesome sectarian, Zwingli now found himself saddled with another. The city council, still troubled about the whole thing, arranged a public disputation, after first imprisoning and torturing Hubmaier.

The exchange was heated. Hubmaier accused Zwingli of inconsistency. He knew of the Reformer's earlier doubts. 'You used to hold the same ideas. Hundreds of people have heard it from your mouth.'[1] Zwingli had to assert that he had been mistaken: 'Rashly accepting that the sign testifies to the faith, we had to attack infant baptism. . . . This error misled me.'[2] In other words he had now made up his mind that baptism did not need to be an expression of the conscious faith of the person baptized: it was a sign of God's promises, not man's acceptance of them. Moreover, he had turned his face from any idea of a separated group of believers, and settled for a continuation of the policy of reforming Christendom from within.

The council felt the same. They had already warned the Reformer not to take his teachings to such extremes that the state–church alliance was broken: 'Then there would spring up disobedience towards the magistrates, disunity, heresy, and the weakening and diminution of the Christian faith.'[3]

Its members issued another edict which threatened banishment to all who refused to have their children baptized. Zwingli went into print with a sustained attack on the troublemakers. His tract *Of baptism* introduced what Calvin would later develop as the 'covenant argument' for infant baptism, but also warned, 'The issue is not baptism, but revolt, faction, heresy.'[4]

The leaders of the Radicals fled the country, to scatter their teaching throughout Europe and to face martyrdom within two years.

For the Reformation leaders now took a grim step. They believed that an abyss was opening up at their feet. They were mocked by the Catholics who jeered, 'We told you so – you have torn apart the seamless robe of Christ. Tear it in two pieces and soon it will be in a hundred fragments.' They were harassed by anxious authorities who warned of

[1] Quoted in Verduin, *The reformers and their stepchildren*, p. 201.
[2] *Ibid.*, p. 202.
[3] *Ibid.*, p. 201.
[4] Williams, *The radical reformation*, p. 131.

the collapse of civil order. They were horrified by the extremes of the wilder fanatics, for when the demands of enthusiasts are refused, they become not less extreme but more. And the outbreak of the 'Peasants' War' in Germany (a popular uprising of aggrieved artisans, quickly crushed) convinced them that their worst fears were really justified. Order was in danger of disappearing and Anabaptism worsened the danger. First Zwingli and then Luther invoked the help of the civil power against the Anabaptists. Using the weapons of imprisonment and banishment, they found that the first only created sympathy and the second only scattered sectarianism more widely. The fateful decision was taken to make 'heresy' a capital offence. Beheading, burning or drowning became the regular punishments for preaching the Radical faith.

Naturally enough, the Radicals reacted. From admiring but chiding the Protestant leaders, they turned to condemning them as antichrist. Members of Anabaptist sects were forbidden to enter a Protestant church building. Any hope of mutual understanding and accommodation was lost. Attitudes about baptism hardened. Several groups had never been totally against paedobaptism but were only opposed to its indiscriminate application to the children of those whom they felt to be unbelievers. Now the gap widened. All paedobaptism came to mean to them 'christening' – the weapon of a fallen church and a discredited Christendom. On the other hand adult baptism came to mean more than a personal act of obedience and loyalty: it became an eloquent way of rejecting Christian sacralism and all it stood for. 'It became principally a matter of separation for the purpose of creating a divided church. Their leaders receive baptism as a sign of separation . . . and the wish to abandon the Papists and the Lutherans,'[1] wrote Henry Bullinger, Luther's successor. 'Live as Christ-like as you please. Only desist from rebaptizing, for

[1] *Corpus reformatorum*, Vol. 91, p. 246.

it is as plain as day that with it you are making a faction,'[1] cried Zwingli.

The accusation was a just one, and the Anabaptists cheerfully admitted it. 'The medieval order can be laid low in no more effective way than by abolishing infant baptism,'[2] claimed Conrad Grebel. 'Infant Baptism is a supporting pillar of the papal order. As long as it is not removed, there can be no Christian congregation,'[3] agreed Hans Sockler, and by 'the papal order' he meant Christendom, whether Catholic or Protestant. 'They fight for Infant Baptism, not out of love for children . . . but in order that they may hold up a false Christendom . . . which is the abomination of desolation,'[4] wrote another bitterly.

The number of imprisonments and executions is impossible to estimate, but in whole areas very popular movements with the sympathy and support of the common people were extinguished.

Not surprisingly, the expectation of suffering became an essential part of Anabaptist teaching, and baptism itself took on a further deep meaning. Not only was it a demonstration of the convert's desire to 'die to self', but it was also a likely route to literal death, or at any rate to physical suffering. 'He that is baptized', wrote Conrad Grebel, combining both thoughts, 'has been planted into the death of Christ. True Christians are sheep among wolves, ready for the slaughter. They must be baptized into anguish and affliction, tribulation, persecution, suffering and death. They must be tried in the fire, and must reap the fatherland of rest, not by killing their bodily enemies but by mortifying their spiritual enemies.'[5]

[1] Quoted in Verduin, *The reformers and their stepchildren*, p. 205.
[2] *Ibid.*, p. 205.
[3] *Mennonite quarterly review*, Vol. 21 (1947), p. 283.
[4] Broadbent, *The pilgrim church*, p. 175.
[5] Verduin, *The reformers and their stepchildren*, p. 260.

It must not be imagined that the reformers themselves now simply relied on civil persecution to settle the issue. It embarrassed and grieved them, and they struggled to meet the Anabaptists' arguments at the higher level of theological debate.

Martin Luther worked out a threefold answer to the Anabaptist case. He classified his own doctrine of paedobaptism. He worked out a theology of the church. And he pursued the idea of *ecclesiola in ecclesia* – a faithful church within the wider church (literally 'a little church within the church').

His great book *The Babylonian Captivity of the Church* dealt with the subject of the Sacraments. He utterly repudiated the Catholic idea of *ex opere operato* (that the power of a sacrament is automatically inherent in it and is 'done in the doing'). Anything which contradicted the basic principle of 'God's grace offered in the Word and received by Faith' was ruthlessly rejected. The Catholic sacraments of penance, matrimony, ordination, extreme unction and confirmation were denied sacramental status at all. Christ had ordained two sacraments for the church: baptism and communion. Communion was cut free from the traditional mass which made it a life-giving miracle dependent upon a priestly act. Luther linked it firmly to faith: it declares the grace of God in the giving of Christ and both stirs up and responds to the faith of the communicant. To this he added a difficult conception of the glorified body of Christ present in every place, and on this issue fell out with Zwingli.

But what of baptism? This too he linked with faith. What justifies the recipient is not the baptism, but faith in the promises of God which are associated with baptism. Those incapable of believing, such as infants, are assisted by the faith of those who bring them to baptism and by the prayers of the Christians who are witnesses. Faith would then be expected to make its appearance in the growing child's developing experience. Moreover, when adult years are reached, the Christian must continually 'carry out his baptism' by dying to sin, and by living in a daily attitude of dependence on Christ.

Luther made the baptismal service an impressive one, which included acts of exorcism, the sign of the cross, the use of salt and the immersion of the child in water. Later he was attracted to the extraordinary proposition that the infant does in fact exercise faith. Insisting rightly enough that saving faith means much more than *fides* ('I give my mental assent') and is *fiducia* ('I surrender myself in trust'), he assented, as Reformed Christianity always has done since, that such faith is itself a gift of God. 'Right faith is a thing wrought by the Holy Ghost in us, which changeth us and turneth us into a new nature. How then can we insist that we know exactly when faith is granted?' he asked. 'We hopefully assume the child to be a believer and thus regenerate. The baptism then strengthens the seed of faith. Daily the sinner drowns the sinful man within him by the renewal of his baptismal vows.'[1]

'Luther thought that Infant Baptism best expressed the true relationship of the sinner to God in the matter of salvation. The helpless child symbolized how the grace of God alone saves man. . . . Since he believed that man, in matters of faith was absolutely helpless even as an adult, that it was a divine miracle . . . it was not difficult for him to accept Infant Baptism.'[2]

But in the long run, as Luther himself explained, 'We bring the child with the conviction and the hope that it will come to faith, and we pray that God will give it faith. But we do not baptize on the strength of this belief, but wholly on the fact that God has commanded it.' He was prepared to leave it at that.[3]

[1] Knaake (Ed.), *Works of Martin Luther* (Muhlenburg Press for Concordia, 1960), Vol. 30, p. 448.

[2] *Ibid.*, p. 476.

[3] *Ibid.*, p. 449.

Luther could not have been very happy with his own rather complicated conclusions on this subject. They show him at his worst, as his magnificently truculent teaching about the nature of faith, the authority of Scripture and the victory of Christ, show him at his best. On the whole, his baptismal teaching has not commended itself to his successors, and is not typical of Protestant thinking. More effective was his doctrine of the church.

This, as he realized, was the real issue with the Anabaptists just as the doctrine of salvation was the real issue with the Catholics. What then is the church? First, he asserted that it most certainly is not the papacy. The claim of the church of Rome to be the one universal and apostolic church was rejected with derision. It had neither preserved the gospel nor imitated the way of life exemplified by the apostles. Secondly, he saw the logic of his own rediscovery of the gospel as the message of salvation received by faith. If the church is to guard, express and propagate that gospel, it must be made up of those who embrace its truths. This led him into difficulties.

It was clear to him that the true church, known only to God, must consist of all those (and only those) who are genuine believers. Could this be expressed in any visible manner? 'The right kind of evangelical order cannot be exhibited among all sorts of people. But those who are determined to be Christians . . . must enrol themselves by name and meet apart for prayer and reading, to baptize and take the sacrament,' he wrote. 'But I have not yet the right people for it.'[1] Precisely! The parish churches as he knew them were full of people making a greater or lesser response to the new understanding of the gospel.

His solution was to place the critical emphasis on the visible order and profession of the church. Thus, wherever the gospel is truly preached and the sacraments are scripturally observed and people with good intentions are hearing

[1] Broadbent, *The pilgrim church*, p. 148.

the preaching and receiving the sacraments, the church is present and functioning, and 'we cannot question that among the mass of people, God has His own little group of true believers, few or many'.[1]

The way in which such churches were to be organized was as *Landeskirchen* – territorial churches. The convictions of the majority in a given area were to determine the universal practice in that area, established by law, and presenting a united front. Those who differed should move to an area where the beliefs of the majority were more acceptable to them. This startling proposition was in fact a possibility in sixteenth-century Europe with its multiplicity of small provinces and city states. Successive areas declared for or against the Reformation and until the religious wars broke out their declarations were generally accepted.

This then was Luther's doctrine of the church. He was perfectly aware that it held a tension within itself. Sometimes he accepted that as inevitable, the tension between ideal and reality. At other times he was depressed and discouraged by its out-working, and irritably envious of the admittedly higher standards adopted by the Anabaptists. Was the choice always to be between a too-inclusive church which compromised its own witness and a too-exclusive church which offered little room for the weak? As a middle way, he pursued a further idea, often referred to as *ecclesiola in ecclesia.* This was an attempt to gather together within the wider church those members who showed convincing signs of true conversion and spiritual growth.

He groped after some system in which true believers among the mass of nominal Lutherans could assemble in private houses as well as gather in the larger congregations, and wondered if a more meaningful observation of communion and baptism might be possible in the private gatherings alone. He even toyed with the idea of separating

[1] Quoted in Broadbent, *The pilgrim church*, p. 148.

church congregations into two groups, with a minister teaching the convinced Christians in the cloister while a chaplain addressed the majority in the church.

As the gap between Lutherans and Radicals widened, these ideas were shelved, but they are thoughts to which members of 'state churches' have often returned. The most striking example is the birth of the 'societies' in eighteenth-century Anglicanism, which were the seed-beds of Methodism.

This, then, was Luther's reply to the Radical challenge. A deeply spiritual view of the true church was combined with a realistic acceptance of the actual situation in Christendom. Faith was pinned to a process of patient teaching and reform. But with it went a dependence upon political powers and geographical organizations. The Radicals were not impressed. Abused and tormented, they continued on their own path of separation and restitution. Scattered and disorganized, they fragmented into a multiplicity of sects. Robbed by death of their best leaders, they sometimes followed fanatics. With little chance of peacefully developing a coherent theology, some drifted into heresy. Thus one wing of the Reformation began to slow down and set in a rigid and worldly position, while the other was in danger of being destroyed by persecution or discredited by fanaticism.

That both dangers were eventually to be avoided was due largely to two remarkable men who now appeared. Each faced the issues of church and baptism. Each made a different response. Each offered a distinctive contribution to the debate. Each has left a mark on every successive generation. Their names are Menno Simons and John Calvin.

7
Mennonites and Calvinists

In 1524 a twenty-eight-year-old Catholic priest was appointed to the curacy of a Dutch church. His name was Menno Simons, and he was destined to do more than any other single man for the survival of the Anabaptists and their recovery from the perils of fanaticism.

He was a thoroughly worldly cleric of the type so common at that time. More interested in drinking and gambling than in the nominal discharge of his duties, he was nevertheless aware of the religious turmoil around him. During Menno's training and ordination, Luther had been thundering his denunciations of the papacy and flooding Europe with his evangelical pamphlets. The general air of questioning and unease affected the newly consecrated priest, and he resolved to avoid reading the Bible 'fearing that if I read I might be misled'.[1] His unease persisted, and within a year he found himself doubting the central mystery of the Catholic priesthood: the sacrifice of the mass. 'Perhaps it was not the Lord's flesh and blood! I confessed this thought and prayed. But I could not rid myself of it.'[2]

He decided to read once through the Bible, and soon became immersed in a fascinated study of its pages. The

[1] Menno Simons's autobiography. Quoted in Broadbent, *The pilgrim church*, p. 186.

[2] *Ibid.*, p. 186.

realization began to dawn upon him, 'We have been deceived.'[1]

The result was a strange one, but just possible in those confused times. He continued as a Catholic priest, but let his sympathy be known for 'Reformation teaching'. Applying himself more seriously to his work, he was a popular curate and built a reputation as an 'evangelical preacher'. Yet he came to see afterwards that there had been no heart-changing experience. The guarded approval he gave to Luther's teaching was no more than mental assent. Lutheranism attracted him, but he occupied a well-paid and pleasant post, and had no wish to make life difficult for himself. Had things continued on their normal course he would either have continued as a priest, or drifted through circumstances into the Lutheran camp to become the type of half-hearted parish minister who was to cause the Reformer such grief and disappointment.

Instead, something happened which shattered his comfortable world. The execution took place in his district of 'a God-fearing pious hero, Sicke Snyder by name, who was beheaded because he had renewed his baptism'.[2] Simons was horrified by the execution, impressed by the martyr's demeanour and most of all intrigued by the odd idea of 'rebaptism'. Searching the Bible again with this in mind, he could find no reference to the baptism of infants. Consultation with his own bishop and advice sought from several Lutherans including Martin Luther himself only confused him. He maintained that they all acknowledged the absence of paedobaptism from Scripture and then all gave different reasons for practising it. The break between Reformers and Radicals had now taken place, and he often found baptism to be the subject of earnest debate within his parish.

[1] *Ibid.*, p. 187.

[2] Menno Simons's autobiography. Quoted in Broadbent, *The pilgrim church*, p. 186.

Anabaptists in fact were spreading into Holland, and the worldly priest with Lutheran leanings was very worried. The moral lives and religious earnestness of those he met impressed him. Yet there was a streak of wildness about them that repelled him. A strong interest in unfulfilled prophecy led them into odd speculations. Dangerous murmurs about setting up the kingdom of God were common among them. Menno had in fact come across a revolutionary wing of the movement destined to scandalize Europe and embarrass saner Anabaptists for a century. The grim work of imprisoning, torturing, burning, garrotting and drowning, which Lutherans and Catholics so enthusiastically organized against the 'heretics', was having a natural enough effect. Some of the Radicals were talking of armed resistance. The death of sober leaders threw power into the hands of unbalanced men. Fiery apocalyptic dreams began to appeal to the persecuted people.

In 1533 the explosion came. The German city of Münster, near the Dutch border, had declared itself Lutheran, expelled its Catholic bishop and then become increasingly influenced by Anabaptists. They were so powerful there that the usual persecution was impossible. The city soon became a refuge for harassed heretics of all types, and the more militant of them flocked there to establish a base for their schemes. Lutherans and Catholics united in an army and, led by the deposed bishop, laid siege to the city. Large numbers of enthusiasts, a lack of sober leadership, imminent danger and a minority of revolutionaries: here were all the ingredients for an outbreak of fanaticism. Jan Matthew, a Dutch baker, and Jan of Leiden, a tailor, both of them paranoiac characters much given to colourful visions and grandiose proclamations, took control of the defenders. They announced the setting up of the New Jerusalem, soon to be rescued from its enemies by the return of Christ. Community of property was introduced, polygamy was permitted and severe laws were enacted and enforced. After two years' siege, the city fell. The leaders were tortured to death and their followers mercilessly punished. Greatly exaggerated accounts of the excesses of the past two years rapidly spread and were eagerly believed. To respectable people, Münster proved that all Anabaptists were red revolutionaries, insane fanatics and immoral libertines.

It was very nearly the death-blow to Anabaptism. A renewal of fierce persecution throughout Europe inevitably followed. What was more harmful, the Radicals had lost the image of respectability and consistent living which had so often won them grudging respect.

These events were only a few miles distant from the perplexed 'evangelical priest' Menno Simons. Even closer at hand, he saw some of his own parishioners infected by the enthusiasm. They took up arms in defiant sympathy with Münster's torment and were viciously put down. He deplored their violence, yet knew the extremity of persecution which had driven them to it. He disowned their fanaticism, yet saw among them a zealous pursuit of truth, an abandonment of earthly comforts and an assurance of God's favour which he himself lacked. Everyone joined together in scandalized condemnation of them, yet he shrewdly suspected that what he always called 'the Münster teaching' was only the lunatic fringe of a movement which by and large held to evangelical truth and promoted godliness of life.

He was now in great mental distress, feeling increasingly drawn to a movement which would involve him in unpopularity at best, and martyrdom at worst. At last, on the final day of 1536, twelve years after entering the priesthood, he made the open break with his old religion, and threw in his lot with the Anabaptists. The visible sign of his decision was the acceptance of 'rebaptism' for himself, and it is interesting to see how he viewed it: 'I have been enlightened by the Lord, converted, have fled from Babylon and entered Jerusalem. Surrendering myself to the Lord with body and soul, I committed myself into His gracious hand.'[1] In other words, he saw baptism as a personal act of faith, a renunciation of a false form of religion, an embracing of the people of God and a taking up of the cross of discipleship.

He accepted baptism at the hands of Obbe Phillips, a leader who had disowned the more flamboyant and violent Anabaptism of the Low Countries and was seeking to encourage others to do the same – with such success that many already referred to themselves as Obberites. Their form of baptism was by pouring water upon the head.

For most of the following year Menno lived quietly, studying the Bible and avoiding trouble. This was not to last long. A group of Obberites, scattered leaderless and discouraged, implored him to organize them and to become their pastor. This plunged him into further hesitation and heart-searching, but after months of reflection he gave in to their request. It was the beginning of years of ceaseless labour, constant journeys, ever-present danger and hair-raising adventure. Having once committed himself to the task, he gave every ounce of energy to it. Before long, the 'Obberites' were the 'Mennonites', and his organizing genius was binding together the scattered congregations in a unity they had never known before.

Menno realized that if his followers were to survive the Münster scandal, four things were necessary. There must be a complete turning from fanaticism and prophetic dreams. There must be a disowning of the use of force, even in self-defence. There must be a visible organization with a trained and qualified ministry. There must be an exercise of discipline within the congregations.

In a sense, he was simply restoring the principles of the banished 'Swiss Brethren'. It was high time. The Radicals

[1] Menno Simons's autobiography. Quoted in Broadbent, *The pilgrim church*, p. 190.

were in serious disarray. Even those who had avoided the excesses of the Low Countries' variety were discovering that 'regenerate membership' is an ideal easier to define than to achieve. A very sympathetic observer nevertheless described their tendency to externalism and rigidity: 'They persuade themselves that as soon as they are received outwardly . . . into their own self-gathered assemblies, they are the holy people of God. Frivolous judgments, self-love and spiritual pride abound.'[1]

It is a criticism with a familiar ring. The hard fact is that enthusiastic Christians who separate from a 'system' very quickly create a new institution of their own which may well be as far from demonstrating the mind of Christ as is the one they have left.

Menno's disciplined organization did not entirely deal with the problem. But it created an honoured and respected movement which still exists in the twentieth century. More than that: the baptist churches which form one of the major world-wide movements of the present day, trace with gratitude to the Mennonites many of these insights to which they have given their own expression. With his system of ministerial succession, interdependence of congregations, and exercise of church discipline, Menno Simons proved that belief in a 'spiritual church' *can* be expressed in practice, and that the replacing of 'sacraments' with 'divine ordinances' of communion and baptism, which reflect the believer's inward state, can offer a unifying and eloquent alternative to a state church sacramental system.

Throughout Simons's lifetime the lesson was ignored. His own life was in constant danger, and it is surprising that he managed to die a natural death at the age of sixty-five. His followers in Germany and the Netherlands were harassed and attacked by Lutherans and Catholics alike. Denmark offered them sanctuary and was thoroughly dis-

[1] Broadbent, *The pilgrim church*, p. 186.

approved of for doing so. They had proved their case, but Europe was not yet ready to admit it.

Europe, in fact, was giving its attention to another reformer who was to lead Protestantism as far to the left as Menno had led Radicalism back to the right. The year that Menno Simons decided to be baptized, John Calvin published his *Institutes of the Christian religion.* When Menno Simons gave in to the pleadings of the Dutch Anabaptists to be their leader, John Calvin was yielding to the pleadings of Farel to lead the reforms at Geneva.

John Calvin represented (and came to lead) second generation Protestantism. Only eight years old when Luther's theses thundered around Europe, he never knew as an adult an undivided Christendom. A choice between two systems was open to him from the beginning. After training for law and priesthood, he made the choice, in a typically calm and irrevocable manner. A 'sudden conversion' to which he gave no date, committed him body, mind and heart to the service of the omnipotent God.

The purpose of this chapter is not to review Calvin's vast theological system in general, but to follow the course he took when it had to be worked out in practical terms at the local church level. For the shy, asthmatic scholar who gave Christian doctrine its most systematic expression, was not permitted to follow a life of letters as he wished. A Frenchman himself, he found himself called to hammer out the implications of his teaching in the Franco-Swiss city of Geneva. He did it to such effect that generations of Christians have looked to that city as their spiritual home.

When he arrived there in 1536 an enormous task faced him. He found the place notoriously lax in morals, ruled by a city council jealous of its powers and inhabited by a populace more eager to throw off Romanism than to embrace anything else. He found some evangelical believers who wished to take reform further than Luther had done, troubled by the claims of Anabaptists and eager to have fellowship with those 'pre-Reformation Protestants' the Waldensians. The relationship of these factors to the church system which he evolved has not always been realized. Though the movement he led became the greatest religious revolutionary force in Europe, Calvin never claimed to be an innovator. Just as his *Institutes* was shaped by the Apostles' Creed and his doctrine of God by Augustine, so it must surely be acknowledged that his system of church discipline owed much to the Anabaptists. The Radical movement as a whole he disliked and distrusted, but he saw the force of many of its criticisms of Lutheran and Zwinglian state-dominated churches. He was groping towards the ideal of a free church in a free state.

He saw the weakness of the optimistic assumption that preaching and sacraments produced a true church. He added the third characteristic of a reformed church: the exercise of spiritual discipline. In doing so, he was emulating the Anabaptists. In doing so he also gained for himself the caricature which has persisted ever since: that of the black-avized dictator who interfered with every life and killed every pleasure. He did this because he grafted the discipline of a 'regenerate church' on to the constitution of a 'comprehensive church'. Defining membership of the church as the total of those who gave approval to a scriptural declaration of faith (not to those who claimed a personal experience of conversion) he then sought to mould them into a pure church.

What of baptism? Calvin not only preserved paedobaptism, but made it a powerful weapon in his appeal both to Catholic and Anabaptist. Dismissing Luther's colourful speculations about the unborn baby's spiritual capacity, and denouncing the Anabaptist emphasis on the personal subjective experience of Christ before baptism, he built all of his case around *the priority of grace*. Rejecting the arguments of those who demanded only the baptism of believers, he wrote, 'The delusion which misleads them is that they would always have the THING to precede the SIGN.'[1] But what precedes either, is the grace of God. It is to that grace that any sacrament should supremely bear witness, not to the subjective condition at the moment of the person who receives it. A sacrament he defined as 'an external sign by which the Lord seals on our consciences His promises of good-will toward us, in order to sustain the weakness of our faith, and we in turn testify our piety towards Him, both before Himself, and before angels as well as men'.[2]

'We in turn' is the crux. Just as in all of life, so in the sacraments, God takes the initiative in approaching us: we in return then respond to him. This, said Calvin really turning the tables on the Anabaptists, is best symbolized by paedobaptism. It does not put the baptismal candidate in the wrong position, but puts God in the right position, as sovereign giver of grace.

In the whole of his baptismal argument the Reformer revealed that his eyes were wide open to the popular appeal of the Anabaptists. He understood their arguments, married the widow of one of their ministers, and set out not only to rebut their claims, but to win back their converts to his own church system. Though he referred to them as 'frenzied spirits' who raise 'great disturbance in the Church on account of paedobaptism'[3] and 'furious madmen' who 'cease not to assail this holy ordinance',[4] he paid them the compliment of closely arguing every one of their beliefs. In doing so, he unconsciously bore witness to the essentially Christian and evangelical nature of his opponents. The principles he contended against are very much the principles of a modern baptist (even a Calvinistic baptist!). Certainly they are not the principles of either lunatics

[1] Calvin, *Institutes*, IV.xvi.21.
[2] *Ibid.*, IV.xiv.1.
[3] *Ibid.*, IV.xvi.1.
[4] *Ibid.*, IV.xvi.10.

or heretics, though in the sixteenth century they were regularly assumed to be both.

The Anabaptist argument reflected in Calvin's writings rested on the discontinuity of the old and new covenants, the need for an evangelical experience to precede an evangelical ordinance, and the essential spirituality of the church as consisting of conscious believers only. Calvin maintained the opposite. First, the old and new covenants are alike in foundation, meaning and purpose: they differ only in the external ordinances of initiation – circumcision for the old covenant, baptism for the new.

Therefore, secondly, since circumcision was administered to infants, even though it is said to symbolize both repentance and faith, so baptism can also be administered in the same condition.

Thirdly, to insist that only those who give what is conceived to be convincing proof of spiritual life are to be members of the church is again to displace grace from its essential position. Scriptures like Romans 6:2–4 and Galatians 3:27–29 do not say, 'Die to sin, put on Christ, and then you may be baptized and regarded as a church member.' They say, 'God in grace has called you by his word expressed in baptism and church fellowship: now make these things real by dying to sin and putting on Christ.'

Very neatly he turned against the Anabaptists their reluctance to say that those who die in infancy before they can choose or reject Christ, are eternally lost. But if they are not lost, they are saved. And did not the actions and words of Christ underline this when he received little children, blessed them and said, 'to such belongs the kingdom of God' (Mk. 10:14)?

Pressed as to what then was the condition of a baptized child, Calvin fell back once more on the priority of grace: 'God . . . sanctifies whom He pleases.'[1] But how can that be? It 'is as possible and easy for Him as it is wondrous

[1] Calvin, *Institutes*, IV.xvi.17.

and incomprehensible for us'.[1] To the further objection that scripturally it is the hearing of the Word that leads to faith (Rom. 10:17), he replied that this is the usual, but not the invariable, way. 'Those, therefore, whom the Lord is to illumine with the full brightness of His light, why may He not, if He so pleases, irradiate at present with some small beam. . . . I would not rashly affirm that they are endued with the same faith which we experience in ourselves, or have any knowledge at all resembling faith (this I would rather leave undecided); but I would somewhat curb the stolid arrogance of those men who, as with inflated cheeks, affirm or deny whatever suits them.'[2]

So the infants of Christian parents are to be baptized for future repentance and faith, while unbaptized adults who are capable of hearing and then believing or disbelieving, are required to display signs of repentance and faith before baptism, as were non-Jews under the old covenant when they approached circumcision.

What benefit does infant-baptism then bring? To the parents it symbolizes the grounds of hope which Christian parents have for their children, filling 'pious breasts with no ordinary joy, urging them more strongly to love their affectionate Parent, when they see that, on their account, He extends His care to their posterity . . . seeing with the bodily eye the covenant of the Lord engraven on the bodies of their children'.[3] To the children it presents a powerful argument in later life for claiming the promises of God and embracing him in penitence and faith: 'Being ingrafted into the body of the Church, they are made an object of greater interest to the other members. Then when they have grown up, they are thereby strongly urged to an earnest desire of serving God.'[4]

[1] Calvin, *Institutes*, IV.xvi.18.
[2] *Ibid.*, IV.xvi.19.
[3] *Ibid.*, IV.xvi.9.
[4] *Ibid.*

The result of these efforts to placate, silence or win back the Radicals was in fact one of Calvin's least-known but most remarkable successes. In French Switzerland thousands of Anabaptists came into the field of Calvinism and had their children baptized. At the same time agreement was reached between Calvinists and many of the Waldensians. These mysterious survivors of medieval 'heresy', practising baptism for both believers and their children, greeted with joy those who had left the doctrines of Rome and had accepted the Word of God. Their younger leaders were fascinated by Calvin's complete and logical system. The older leaders admired much of it but held aloof from formal amalgamation. The two groups parted company, the younger bringing its wealth of experience into the Reformer's camp and experiencing itself something akin to a religious revival.

Within a century Calvinism had replaced Anabaptism as the most influential expression of Christianity in the Low Countries, and had become the persecuted but defiant Protestantism of France and Scotland, and the Christian orthodoxy of England and her colonies. The whole content of the baptismal controversy had altered. In the Middle Ages paedobaptism stood for Catholicism, and adult baptism for evangelical 'heresy'. During the Lutheran Reformation, paedobaptism symbolized state Christianity, and adult baptism symbolized voluntary Christianity. Through Calvin's reforms, paedobaptism came to represent a predestinarian view of the gospel, while adult baptism accompanied a strong emphasis on human free-will. As we showed in Part one, many would claim that this has remained the basic baptismal issue ever since.

8
The politician and the pot-mender

The Puritan era in England was an age that made legends. Like most legends they tend to the caricature rather than the literal truth. The very word 'Puritan' conjures up in many minds a picture of tall-hatted, long-faced, psalm-singing spoil-sports, full of cant and hypocrisy. To others, the Puritans are the most apostolic men the world has known since the apostles themselves.

'There were giants in the earth in those days' (Gn. 6:4, AV), and their names were household words. Seraphic Thomas Watson drew crowds to his parish church weekly to hear thirty-point sermons. Stern-faced John Owen's sonorous phrases held Parliament spell-bound and influenced the nation's affairs. Warm-hearted Richard Baxter set every family in Kidderminster praying.

John Brown defied a ruthless king to establish the right of humble folk to worship God as their consciences dictated. John Smyth's restless mind drove him from Anglican to Presbyterian to Independent to Anabaptist, and produced the first English statement of religious toleration. Stocky John Bunyan preached to village congregations what he 'smartingly did feel' and made his prison the birth-place of a religious classic. William Roger's pulpit pleadings threw hundreds of Essex hearers into a paroxysm of tears. Thomas Hooker's market-day lectures sharply reduced the crime rate in Chelmsford. And over the whole scene strode the massive and enigmatic figure of Cromwell, forcing democracy on a Parliament that suspected it, forcing godliness on a nation that rejected it and forcing tolerance on a religion that denounced it.

Equally gigantic was the royal family of Stuart: four successive kings with a remarkable aptitude for choosing the wrong side. It cost one of them his head and another his throne. It hounded evangelicals to death or exile, and twice drove them in desperation to revolution.

It is not surprising that this was an age of intolerance. Mutual tolerance is one of the very few features of twentieth-century Christianity in which it could claim to be an improvement on the seventeenth century. On the other hand, the people of the Puritan era took their souls and their God very seriously indeed: an attitude which twentieth-century man finds distinctly puzzling.

Two men stood out as particularly glowing examples of both intense conviction and broad tolerance. They looked at the baptism, as well as other points of controversy, and perhaps brought it nearer to a solution than anyone before or since. Their names were John Owen and John Bunyan. To understand their contribution to the debate we must take a rapid look at the circumstances of their time.

Church of England was the religion of the realm, by law established. The church occupied a position definitely Protestant in doctrine, but in many ways Catholic in structure and practice. Every citizen was legally required to be baptized as an infant, to be confirmed as an adult and to attend public worship at an Anglican church. It was a perfect example of the 'sacralist society'.

Within the ranks of Anglicanism were growing numbers of 'Puritans' who wished to retain a state church but were dissatisfied with its current condition, and bent on transforming it from within. Looking to Calvin's Geneva as their ideal, they aimed for a Calvinistic system of doctrine and a presbyterian system of church government. Outside its ranks were the Dissenters or Separatists. They (on the whole) accepted Geneva's doctrine, but believed that it contradicted Geneva's practice. To them a pure and scriptural church must of necessity have a regenerate membership, and this meant the end of a state church. They gathered groups of Christians on the basis of a personal confession of faith, and regarded them and their children alone as members of the true church. They became the Independents or Congregationalists of later denominational life. In turn some of them took the logic further: 'Surely,' they said, 'regenerate membership leads to the baptism of believers only, and the rebaptism of those merely christened as infants.' Some were influenced by Dutch Mennonites and, discarding their Calvinistic theology, became 'General Baptists'. Others (the majority) preserved the theology of Geneva and became 'Particular Baptists'. The wheel had turned full circle. Calvinism had led to Anabaptism.

Steering a dangerous course throughout this era and among these divided Christians was the universally respected figure of John Owen, 'the Calvin of England'. He was converted at Oxford University, and from the beginning gave his immense mind to the statement and defence of Reformation doctrine. Manoeuvred out of college by High-Church enemies, he worked quietly as a chaplain until the outbreak of the Civil War, and then became rector of two successive Essex villages. At Fordham he was a Presbyterian, working hopefully within the established church. By the time he reached Coggleshall in 1646, he had come to Independent convictions, and wished to pastor a separated group of convinced Christians.

Nevertheless, it was here that he pioneered a remarkable idea for combining a state system and a voluntary system of church government. He suggested an arrangement whereby ministers could fulfil a double function as 'rector' of a typically mixed parish and 'pastor' of groups within the parish of those who professed conversion and met as 'gathered churches'.

The scheme never really got off the ground outside Essex, but it showed how Owen's mind was working: he wished to see division among Christians reduced to an absolute minimum. As his influence grew, and he became preacher to Parliament, chaplain to Cromwell and Vice-Chancellor of Oxford University, he nursed his dream of evangelical unity. The Christians he met everywhere were essentially one in belief. They all bore the three classic marks of a true church – preaching of the truth, administration of the sacraments and exercise of discipline.

'Nor shall any man be able to prove but that, on the doctrinal agreement which we all profess, we may, notwithstanding the differences that remain, enjoy all that peace and union which are prescribed into the churches and disciples of Christ.'[1] In this he quite clearly included 'moderate' Anglicans, Presbyterians, Congregationalists *and Baptists*. His very affection for John Bunyan makes this clear, and many of his other actions underline the fact. This was in striking contrast to some of his colleagues, who regarded Baptists with unconcealed dislike, and labelled them 'Anabaptists' with all the unpleasant connotations of that word.

Saintly Thomas Watson, for example, staunch Presbyterian whose ministry at St Stephen's, Walbrook, was deeply effective in the heart of London, dropped all of his customary good sense and biblical argument when preaching on baptism: 'The baptism of persons grown up to maturity we may argue against from the ill consequences of it. They dip the persons they baptize over head and ears in cold water and naked, which is as indecent as it is

[1] Goold (Ed.), Owen, *Collected works* (Banner of Truth, 1965–66), Vol. 15, p. 220.

dangerous.'[1] Thus, he solemnly concluded, by being baptized naked (which of course they were not), the candidates encouraged immoral thoughts and thus broke the seventh commandment, while by encouraging them to do so, their ministers made them liable to catch cold and die, thus breaking the sixth commandment. Those who do these things are people of 'vile opinions and vicious practices' while their unbaptized children are 'sucking pagans'.[2] With debate at that kind of level, it is not surprising that any friendly spirit, let alone reconciliation, seemed impossible.

Yet in such a context, John Owen, probably the most widely-read and influential of the Puritan theologians was advocating the closest possible co-operation and the avoidance of hostility and distrust. He went further, and proposed intercommunion: the mutual acceptance of Christians at one another's celebration of the Lord's Supper. 'Where any . . . make confession of that truth whereby they may abide in Christ and are preserved from pernicious seductions, although they may differ from us and the truth in some things of less moment, we are obliged not only to *forbearance* of them, but *communion* with them. For who shall refuse those whom Christ hath received? This and no other is the rule of our evangelical love and communion among ourselves. Whatever we require more . . . is an unwarrantable imposition on their consciences or practice.'[3]

In 1654 Oliver Cromwell became Protector of the Commonwealth and head of state in an England which five years earlier had executed its king. One of the first results was his own remarkable attempt to achieve a just solution of the religious problems. He created what must surely be the most elastic state church ever conceived.

[1] Watson, *The ten commandments* (Banner of Truth, 1962), p. 221.
[2] *Ibid.*, p. 163.
[3] Owen, *Collected works*, Vol. 4, p. 147. Italics ours.

Supported by public taxes, its clergy were appointed by 'Triers' responsible to Parliament. The only qualifications required of a minister were evangelical soundness of doctrine and evidence of a consistent character. Within those limits, he could be a Presbyterian, an Independent or a Baptist and could lead his congregation in any of these paths. Prominent on the Board of Commissioners in charge of the whole complex scheme was John Owen. He must have been very happy indeed to serve in that capacity, for the scheme embodied principles which he had repeatedly advocated, and his influence is undoubtedly apparent in many of its details.

In the town of Bedford, a little group of hitherto despised Christians was quick to grasp a dazzling opportunity. About two dozen were gathered together as a 'Gospel Church'. Under the leadership of John Gifford, an ex-Royalist Army Officer turned disreputable doctor and then dramatically converted, they had met quietly as a separatist church through all the recent troubled years 'without any form and order as to visible church communion . . . zealous to edify themselves and to propagate the Gospel . . . showing their detestation of the bishops and their superstitions'.[1] It is curiously difficult to decide whether they constituted an Independent or a Baptist church, and the two denominations have had friendly arguments ever since as to which of them can claim the humble tinker who was to become the group's most illustrious member.

'The principle upon which they thus entered into fellowship one with another and upon which they did afterwards receive those that were added . . . was faith in Christ and holiness of life, without respect to this or that circumstance or opinion in outward and circumstantial things.'[2] So reads their own earliest account. They seem to have

[1] *The Bunyan meeting book.* Quoted in Brittain, *In the steps of John Bunyan* (Rich & Cowan, 1950), p. 145.

[2] *Ibid.*, p. 146.

regarded the issue of baptism as such an 'outward and circumstantial thing'. Conscience and Scripture apparently led them to hold believers' baptism by immersion as the ideal, and a little inlet of the River Ouse 'beneath an elm-tree near the corner of Duck Mill Lane'[1] was their baptistry. However, they did not demand the ideal. Christians already baptized as infants in the established church could be received into membership of this group, and members who wished to have their children baptized seem to have been free to take them to the parish church for that purpose. It was an extraordinary attitude at that time, when Anglicans despised and oppressed Dissenters, when Independents regarded Anglicans as members of Antichrist and Baptists demanded rebaptism and a complete disowning of every other denominational affiliation.

Suddenly this little group found itself respectable. The Rector of St John's, Bedford was ejected. Dissenter John Gifford passed the scrutiny of the Triers with flying colours, and found himself established as the new rector, with full permission to use the parish church for his flock and his faith. The same year there called at the rectory a troubled tinker named John Bunyan. For at least three years this rough labourer in his mid-twenties had been undergoing agonies of spiritual conflict. Possessed of a remarkable imagination, he clothed his thoughts with such vivid imagery that he heard and saw them as voices and visions. His spiritual pilgrimage was a long one, which drove him to the verge of mental breakdown, before he found inner peace under Gifford's ministry. He was baptized under the elm tree and registered as number twenty-six on the church membership roll.

Before long he was a famous preacher. Before long, too, Cromwell was dead, Charles II was on the throne and a cavalier Parliament was bent on revenge against the Puritans. In 1660 John Owen was expelled from Oxford

[1] *Ibid.*, p. 149.

and formed an Independent church in London. John Bunyan was to receive rougher treatment: twelve years in prison as an illegal preacher. From his prison cell his books began to pour. The imagination which had once hounded his conscience now flowered into an astonishing ability to write books which lit up the Bible and searched the heart to its depths.

Meanwhile, the Great Ejection in 1662 hurled two thousand Puritan ministers of the Church of England into expulsion, homelessness and harassment. At the same time it ensured the survival of religious dissent in England. At one blow, the small and despised congregations of Independents and Baptists were joined by many of the most spiritual and intellectual of the Anglican clergy in a common nonconformist exile, while thousands of the most influential and educated members followed their ejected ministers. By 1672 the King had accepted the impossibility of crushing dissent even with the most savage legislation and for a mixture of reasons insisted on a Declaration of Indulgence which permitted a limited freedom. John Bunyan promptly applied for a licence to preach. The Bedford Meeting which had survived ten years of underground activity invited him to be their pastor, and permission was granted him.

The new pastor had been given plenty of time in prison to ponder on what is really essential to Christianity. He had a moving last letter from dying John Gifford to his beloved church to ponder on too: 'Concerning separation from the Church about baptism, laying on of hands, anointing with oils, psalms, or any externals, I charge every one of you as you will give account of it to our Lord Jesus Christ . . . that none of you be found guilty of this great evil.'[1] It is this striking definition of baptism as an 'external' and its relegation to the ranks of varying local practices prevalent among dissenting churches, that Bunyan con-

[1] Brittain, *In the steps of John Bunyan*, p. 157.

tinued to accept. It was the key to his own church discipline and to the relationship of his church with other Christian bodies. It led him into a good deal of criticism. That same year his infant son was baptized at the parish church presumably at the wish of his wife, who never became a member of the Bedford Meeting. John was rapidly becoming a nationally known figure, and was generally regarded as a Baptist. His stricter Baptist colleagues became thoroughly alarmed at his 'compromising' attitude both in family and church life and a book appeared on the subject. Written by two well-known Baptist ministers, Paul and Kiffin, it was called *Some Serious Reflections on that Part of Mr Bunyan's Confession of Faith Touching Church Communion with Unbaptized Persons.*

The Confession referred to, built its scheme of fellowship on the words of Romans 15:7, 'Welcome one another, therefore, as Christ has welcomed you.' It was too simplified an approach for enthusiastic Baptists, and they roundly castigated him in the abusive language normally employed in seventeenth-century religious debate. A swift reaction came from John's pen, called *Differences in Judgment on Water Baptism No Bar to Communion.* It was a trenchant reply to their criticism and a ringing call to love and tolerancc. It was built on two principles: *only* God's people make up a local church, but *all* of God's people should be included.

What then of baptism? John was explicit: 'Touching shadowish or figurative ordinances. . . . I believe that Christ hath ordained but two in His Church, *viz.* Water Baptism and the Supper of the Lord. But *I count them not as fundamentals* of our Christianity. Servants they are . . . to teach and instruct us in the weighty matters. . . . It is possible to commit idolatry, even with God's own appointments.'[1] But can the Christian act of initiation really be

[1] Offor (Ed.), *The works of John Bunyan* (Blackie & Son, 1848), Vol. 2, p. 604.

considered 'not a fundamental'? He went on to a robust denial that baptism is in fact initiation. It is not the new covenant equivalent of circumcision. From Romans 2:28, 29 and Philippians 3:1–4 he argued that the new covenant 'circumcision' is a renewed heart and a right spirit. 'He is not a real Jew who is one outwardly, nor is true circumcision something external and physical. He is a Jew who is one inwardly, and real circumcision is a matter of the heart, spiritual and not literal. His praise is not from men but from God.'

'We are the true circumcision, who worship God in spirit, and glory in Christ Jesus, and put no confidence in the flesh.'

So initiation is not baptism, but the inward change of heart which begins the Christian life. Baptism is merely the outward sign of that inward change, and whether and how to be baptized are personal acts of obedience. To regard baptism as a church sacrament is to lift the baptismal controversy into an area where it is bound to confuse and divide. In that case, 'If Water Baptism . . . trouble their peace, wound the consciences of the godly, dismember and break their fellowship: it is, although an ordinance, for the present TO BE PRUDENTLY SHUNNED . . ., for the edification of the Church is to be preferred before it.'[1]

This was strong stuff, and of course it opened the Bedford pastor to the charge that he was trying to resolve the baptismal problem, not with a baptismal theology, but with a non-theology. *How Long is it Since You Were a Baptist*? asked the next pamphlet to be issued, and in his further reply, entitled *Peaceable Principles and True*, Bunyan gave the spirited reply that he was happy to leave the title 'Baptist' with the only man to whom the Bible gives it – John the Baptist. As far as John Bunyan was concerned: 'Since you would know by what name I would be distinguished from others; I tell you, I would be and hope I

[1] *Ibid.*, Vol. 2, p. 609.

am a Christian. As for these factious titles of Anabaptists, Independents, Presbyterians or the like, I conclude that they came neither from Jerusalem nor Antioch, but rather from Hell and Babylon, for they naturally tend to divisions.'[1]

John Owen was well aware of these opinions. He had long admired his less academic but more eloquent fellow-minister, and had used his influence in court and church circles to hasten Bunyan's release from prison. The tinker had shown his *Pilgrim's Progress* to the statesman, who was so impressed that he sent it on to his own publisher. He also intended to write an Introduction to Bunyan's defence of his baptismal practice but was dissuaded by other Baptists. The universal church is the loser. *Owen on Baptism* is a treasure we can ill afford to do without. Bunyan accepted the disappointment philosophically. 'Perhaps it is more for the glory of God that truth should go naked into the world, than as seconded by so mighty an armour-bearer as he.'[2]

In any case, events were pressing Christians into a unity of sympathy and purpose greater than any denominational division. James II succeeded his brother Charles to the throne, and a king with a secret sympathy for the papacy was replaced by a king who openly espoused Roman Catholicism. The Church of England found itself as harassed as the dissenters. The Archbishop of Canterbury and six bishops were imprisoned and on trial. Dissenting ministers visited them in prison and knelt in prayer with their arms around them. A common Protestantism was now at stake, and divided Christians closed their ranks. Included in the movement towards closer evangelical fellowship were both Calvinistic and Arminian Baptists, threatened by persecution without and false doctrine within. They began to see (and to admit) that a paedobaptist who is

[1] *Ibid.*, Vol. 2, p. 649.
[2] *Ibid.*, Vol. 2, p. 649.

orthodox is more to be welcomed than a Baptist who is heretical. It is a proposition to which evangelical baptists in the twentieth century would give hearty assent.

By that time the country, sickened by a century of conflict, said, 'Away with the royal family and their religion: we want a Protestant nation and freedom of conscience.' By that time, too, Christians had learnt their need of each other. If they could not reconcile their differences, they could hold them in love and mutual respect. For Nonconformists (with the exception of the Strict Baptist Movement) the intercommunion for which John Owen had contended became increasingly common. More and more Christians gave their approval to John Bunyan's declaration: 'I will not let water baptism be the rule, the door, the bolt, the bar, the wall of division between the righteous and the righteous.'[1]

[1] *Ibid.*, Vol. 2, p. 656.

9
Two centuries

The end of the Puritan era saw the end of the baptismal controversy. Not, of course, that the controversy was settled, but that the issues having been raised, the lines of division were thereafter drawn in an increasingly permanent way. Christians became either infant or adult baptists, mutually exclusive and hence ignorant, suspicious and intolerant of each other's practice and belief. From time to time, movements of religious revival raised again the problems associated with different baptismal positions, and sometimes possible solutions to the controversy were proposed. Not, however, until the twentieth century did baptism become, once more, a subject of major importance to the whole of the Christian church.

Methodism and the Evangelical Awakening

The Evangelical Awakening in the eighteenth century was one of the most astonishing forward surges of the Christian church. Bringing new life and enthusiasm to the formal Christianity of England, Scotland, Wales and the American colonies, its influence was decisive at a time when the Anglo-Saxon peoples were beginning to shape the course of world history. The widespread Methodist movement was one result of a work of revival which swept tens of thousands of converts into the churches, deepened the life and witness of every denomination and purged Britain of many of the ills and injustices which had brought her to the brink of revolution.

At first sight, baptism does not seem to have been an issue in those exciting times. But a closer look reveals that every one of the great leaders of the revival had a hard tussle with the subject. The question which arose was not so much 'Who should be baptized?' but 'What does it accomplish?' For the double rediscovery that was made by the great evangelists was, first, the doctrine of justification by faith alone, and second, the possibility of a present subjective experience of pardon and assurance. The heart-experience of John Wesley, 'strangely warmed', was echoed in the life of every one of the leaders. George Whitefield in England, Howell Harris in Wales, William Tennant in America, Peter Bohler of Germany, all found the same great assurance, and preached it to thronging thousands.

> Thine eye diffused a quickening ray, –
> I woke, the dungeon flamed with light;
> My chains fell off, my heart was free,
> I rose, went forth, and followed Thee.[1]

So they sang, for so it had happened.

This change was referred to in its scriptural terms of 'conversion', 'new birth' and 'regeneration'. It was the fundamental and distinctive doctrine of the whole great movement. But the very terms used raised a painful problem. Most of the leaders of first and second rank were faithful sons of the Church of England. Throughout their lives they struggled to remain within the Anglican fold and to keep their converts there. Their 'societies', which in the next generation became separate Methodist or Presbyterian churches, were at first simply groups of converts within the established church, forming an *ecclesiola in ecclesia*. Yet here

[1] Charles Wesley, *The Methodist hymn book*, no. 371.

came the difficulty. At the very heart of the service for Infant Baptism in the Prayer book which they acknowledged and used, were the words, 'Seeing . . . dearly beloved . . . that this child is regenerate. . . .'

If the great majority of their hearers had been regenerated in infancy through baptism, how could they press upon them their present need for regeneration through repentance and faith in Christ?

George Whitefield, who pioneered evangelistic preaching in churches and in the open air, well knew the danger of dependence on ecclesiastical ceremonies. Only a long struggle had freed him from it. 'God showed me that I must be born again, or be damned! I learnt that a man may go to church, say his prayers, receive the sacrament, and yet not be a Christian. How did my heart rise and shudder!'[1] '(But) oh what joy unspeakable filled my soul when the weight of sin went off, and an abiding sense of the pardoning love of God broke in upon my disconsolate soul!'[2]

In the first sermon preached after his ordination he caused a sensation by pressing the need for an immediate conscious conversion to Christ. He expounded and distinguished the meanings of the phrase 'in Christ'. First, we can be said to be in Christ by outward profession through being baptized into Christ's church. But in fact with most people this has little consequence: church life is either ignored or formally observed. So those who have been 'born of water' in baptism must also be 'born of the Spirit' in conversion – or to employ John the Baptist's phrase in place of Christ's, those who have merely been 'baptized with water' need to be 'baptized with the Holy Ghost'.

This approach was adopted by many of the revival preachers, especially if, like Whitefield, their theology was Puritan and Calvinistic. They saw baptism in covenantal terms, were embarrassed by the use of the word regenera-

[1] Dallimore, *George Whitefield* (Banner of Truth, 1970), p. 73.
[2] *Ibid.*, p. 77.

tion in connection with it and would have preferred its application in infancy to be limited to the children of godly parents.

> God seals to saints His glorious grace
> And not forbids their infant-race.
> Their seed is sprinkled with His blood,
> Their children set apart for God,
> His Spirit on their offspring shed,
> Like water poured upon the head.[1]

When such preachers mentioned baptism they usually had one of two purposes. Either it had a negative lesson: a warning that no external ceremony, however sacred, could change the human heart or remove the need for a personal encounter with Christ. Or it had a positive lesson: the memory of baptism stood as a visible and objective pledge from God that he who received and blessed an unconscious and undeserving infant is equally willing to receive and forgive the vilest outcast who cries to him for mercy.

The approach of John and Charles Wesley was curiously different. They felt more bound by the Book of Common Prayer than most of their contemporaries and most of their converts. When touching upon baptism, John often used the dutiful phrase 'our Church supposes' or 'it is the teaching of our Church'. Before his own conversion he firmly believed in 'baptismal regeneration' as he saw it taught in a church which, in the words of Lord Chatham, had Calvinistic Articles, Arminian ministers and a Romish liturgy.

After his conversion he saw that this would not do. His solution was completely original. At baptism, he suggested, infants are born again of the Holy Spirit and cleansed from inherited sin. But as a matter of observed fact, each then grows into a life of personal sin and rejects the grace of God, thus forfeiting the eternal life granted in baptism.

[1] George Whitefield. Quoted in Holland, *Baptism in early Methodism* (Epworth, 1970), pp. 122, 123.

Each then needs to be regenerated a second time by adult conversion. We need, as it were, to be born again, again![1]

Charles Wesley embraced this idea, and expressed it quite clearly in some of his hymns.

> When e'er the pure baptismal rite
> Is duly ministered below,
> The heavens are opened in our sight
> And God His Spirit doth bestow;
> The grace infused invisible
> Which would with man forever dwell.
>
> But oh, *we lost the grace bestowed*,
> Nor let the Spirit on us remain;
> Made void the ordinance of God,
> By sin *shut up the heavens again*,
> Who would not keep our garments white
> Or walk as children of the light.[2]

It made an effective instrument in evangelism. When John Wesley cried to Anglican hearers, 'Lean no more on the staff of that broken reed, that ye were born again in baptism,' his emphasis was on the word *were*.[3] He did not mean that their baptism was ineffective *at the time*: he meant that they had rendered it ineffective *since*.

At the same time, both of the Wesleys were quite busy baptizing adults, as an outcome of their evangelistic journeys. They would never rebaptize those already christened in infancy within the Church of England. But they cheerfully dismissed the baptism of infants by Nonconformists, and thus treated alike converts not baptized at all and those baptized as infants in dissenting chapels. Many a riverbank was the scene of enthusiastic baptismal services conducted by the Wesleys. Some they baptized

[1] See Holland, *Baptism in early Methodism*, ch. 6.

[2] Quoted in Holland, *Baptism in early Methodism*, p. 67.

[3] Sugden (Ed.), *Wesley's standard sermons* (Epworth, 1921), Vol. 1, p. 296.

because they had experienced conversion: others were baptized as anxious enquirers in *order* to be converted, and often as they emerged from the water, 'God filled their hearts with peace and joy unspeakable in that very moment.'[1]

Not surprisingly, the Baptists used these events to strengthen their own case for the universal need of adult baptism. Numbers of Methodist societies became Baptist churches, and Charles Wesley, furious with this 'carnal, cavilling, contentious sect, always watching to steal away our children and make them as dead as themselves',[2] prevailed on his brother to write *A Treatise on Baptism – a Preservative against Unsettled Notions in Religion.* This leaflet defended the double practice of infant and adult baptism.

This story may seem a mere side-issue of the great revival, and perhaps it is. Yet it underlines the problem which baptism always must raise with the evangelical Christian. And the attempts to solve it in the eighteenth century created consequences which are still with us. Within the Church of England, the Evangelical Party preserved Whitefield's approach, and this was to lead a century later to great conflict with Anglo-Catholics about 'baptismal regeneration'. Wesleyan Methodists were unimpressed by the Wesleys' theory of baptism, and instead adopted a very casual approach to the sacrament. The words 'this child is regenerate' disappeared and were replaced by a non-committal formula which has led to the oft-repeated assertion that every Methodist minister has his own view of what baptism means. The Baptists made phenomenal progress in the American colonies as a result of the preaching of Whitefield and his colleagues, with the result that their churches found themselves in the role of a major denomination in Christendom for the first time.

[1] Curnock (Ed.), *The journal of the Rev. John Wesley* (1909), Vol. 6, p. 49, for one of many similar examples.

[2] Jackson (Ed.), *Wesleyan minister: Memoirs of the Rev. Charles Wesley* (1848), Vol. 2, p. 128.

10
The missionary movements

The Evangelical Awakening of the eighteenth century led in turn to a great period of expansion for Protestant and evangelical Christianity throughout the world in the nineteenth century. Though it coincided with, and owed something to, the parallel expansion of European culture and 'colonialism', it was certainly not an automatic accompaniment to it. Indeed, much European Christianity was purely nominal except when touched by times of revival. Very many Europeans discarded it when they emigrated. Much of the spirit of their colonial expansion was flatly contrary to the spirit of the gospel, and made evangelism more difficult. 'The spread of Christianity in connexion with the expansion of Europe was chiefly through minorities, sometimes small minorities, who committing themselves fully to it, became expressions of the abounding vitality inherent in the Gospel.'[1]

One distinctive factor in this forward move was that it carried the denominational differences of Europe (and particularly Britain) with it. This is easy to criticize now, but it is difficult to see how it could have been avoided at the time. Conversions eventually came in a flood, but only after long periods when the missionaries laboured on alone and unencouraged. William Carey, the pioneer of them all,

[1] Latourette, *A history of Christianity*, p. 924.

had to wait seven years for his first convert in India. Missionaries on the West Coast of Africa, with an average life expectancy of eighteen months, sometimes died without seeing one result. Naturally enough, they practised Christianity in the way they were used to it: it was a link with home in a hostile land.

Baptists were first in the field, with the Baptist Missionary Society opening up India in 1792 and then the Congo basin in Africa. Congregationalists of the London Missionary Society reached the South Pacific in 1795, and Presbyterians of the Scottish Missionary Society made Africa their target a year later. Anglicans of the Church Missionary Society were in Africa by the last year of the century, and seventeen years later the Wesleyan Methodist Missionary Society had reached the West Indies. By 1815 American Protestantism was also reaching out with a zeal and vision which would ultimately enable the Americans to replace the British as the major source of funds and personnel for world evangelism.

Naturally, all of the missionary societies practised adult baptism. That is to say, they often had occasion to baptize adult converts. They were in a replica of the apostolic situation. Yet even in the first generation the old divisions reappeared, for all except baptists were willing to baptize adult converts *and their children.* Indeed, when mass movements emerged, Anglicans and Presbyterians were willing to baptize whole villages or areas. The result was that areas of the world adopted a Christianity where baptismal practices depended on the denominational source from which the pioneer missionaries came. The 'average' Christian in Zaïre today is very likely to have been baptized as an adult believer. His counterpart in East Africa will have received paedobaptism.

A second missionary era began when evangelicalism was on the wane in Europe and America. Suspecting the liberal or sacramental tendencies which were gaining ground in the older denominations, a new generation of missionaries established the great 'faith missions'. These were organized outside of the denominational leadership, and drew support from evangelicals across the whole spectrum of Protestantism. So for example, Hudson Taylor's work led to the foundation of the China Inland Mission, C. T. Studd's to the forming of the Worldwide Evangelization Crusade. The many societies like them had no denominational pattern to import to the 'mission-field'. They concentrated on building indigenous churches and handing them the Scriptures as quickly as possible. As a matter of plain fact, the result has usually been the establishment of adult baptism as the norm.

The Brethren movement

The Brethren movement began in the 1830s, as the expression of a desire for true spiritual unity in Christ. The early leaders like J. N. Darby and George Müller believed that the truth of the Body of Christ was confused and denied by the existence of separate organized denominations and the creation within Christendom of a separate class of clergy. Their desire for Christians to worship together solely on the basis of their fellowship with Christ, struck a chord in many hearts, and without any visible organization or appointed leadership, the idea spread rapidly. However, from the beginning there were differences of approach which made eventual division inevitable.

Those who, like Müller, became known as 'Open Brethren' saw their duty as a recovery of New Testament principles and practice. The gradual clarification of what they believed this to mean brought them to the baptist position; they saw the pattern to be independent assemblies of believers, practising only believers' baptism. Their opposition to ordained clergy kept them separate from Baptists in Britain and America and wherever their missionaries did their immensely fruitful work on every continent. Movements closely akin to them emerged: the 'Little Flock' of China and the Bakht Singh movement of India. In Germany and Russia, under the pressure of hostile government, they have found their views on baptism sufficiently close to enter into union with Baptists and Pentecostals in the twentieth century.

Darby's approach to the rebuilding of the New Testament church was very different. He saw such an effort to be a misunderstanding of the situation. Answering the question, 'Are Christians competent to form organized churches after the model of the primitive churches?' he replied, 'No! For the Church is in a state of ruin. . . . The first departure is fatal . . . the Scripture never recognizes a recovery from such a state.'[1] What then should troubled Christians do? 'They ought to meet in the unity of the Body of Christ outside the world, taking heed of the promise of Christ that where two or three gather together in His Name, He is present.'[2] One curious result of this approach was that the Exclusive Brethren (who accepted Darby's view) adopted from the beginning an approach to baptism which promised to resolve many of the difficulties between paedobaptists and baptists.

Baptism, they suggested, is always and only connected with visible profession and admission to external privilege. It brings the baptized, not into the enjoyment of forgiveness, regeneration, *etc.*, but into the circle of Christian profession where these things are taught and sought. 'Believers' baptism', they pointed out, is no more a biblical expression than 'infant baptism'. An adult person is properly baptized *for* the remission of sins, *to* put on Christ, and is buried with Christ *by* baptism (Acts 2:38; Gal. 3:27; Rom. 6:4). 'The really important moment as to baptism for us as believers is when we realize what is

[1] Broadbent, *The pilgrim church*, pp. 374, 375.

[2] *Ibid.*, p. 377.

involved in it, and accept in our souls that to which we were committed in baptism. We are baptized not because we are saved but because we are lost.'[1]

As far as the baptism of infants was concerned, Exclusive Brethren maintained the principle of 'household baptism' and accepted whole-heartedly the classic reformed arguments for it. If Jesus is Lord to a new convert, then 'Jesus is Lord to all his household, whose members are thus introduced to the outward circle of profession and privilege of Christianity'[2]. Though this approach implies only the baptism of believers and their children, Exclusive Brethren generally recognize indiscriminate infant baptism as an existential fact often prevailing outside of their own ranks, and neither demand nor favour rebaptism in these cases. On the other hand, if a convert already baptized in infancy feels troubled in conscience and asks for adult baptism, this is normally made possible.

Because of other developments within their ranks, the teachers of this view are scarcely known or listened to by other Christians. This is to everyone's loss, for the fact is that they have found a successful way of combining the regular practice of adult baptism and believers' baptism within an evangelistic framework, and with room for freedom of conscience in the sticky matter of rebaptism.

Modern developments

While the Exclusive Brethren were finding their own solution to the baptismal controversy, opinion in the older churches continued to harden. In June 1864 Charles Haddon Spurgeon, perhaps the most outstanding Nonconformist minister of the whole nineteenth century, preached a celebrated sermon on the subject of baptismal regeneration. His target was not so much the practice of

[1] *Letters of C. A. Coates* (Stow Hill Bible and Tract Depot), p. 33.
[2] *Ibid.*

paedobaptism itself as the position then being asserted by the leaders of the Tractarian Movement in the Church of England that salvation was effected only through baptism. Spurgeon's language was uncompromising: 'Out of any system which teaches salvation by baptism must spring infidelity, ...which the false Church already seems willing to nourish and foster beneath her wing. God save this favoured land from the brood of her own established religion!'[1]

Not surprisingly, Spurgeon's language was repaid in kind as a stream of tracts and counter-tracts appeared, reminiscent in the bitterness of their language of the earlier conflicts between Reformers and Anabaptists. By the end of the century Anglo-Saxon Christians were either firmly infant or adult baptist and knew definitely the reasons why. So great was the mutual hostility between them that it was unthinkable for an adult baptized in infancy to consider rebaptism as a believer, while Baptists could be expelled from their churches for attending an infant baptismal service!

Only with the coming of the twentieth century has the climate of opinion changed and, paradoxically, has baptism become once more a major issue, not now of controversy, but of debate among all Christians. The following are among factors which have brought about this change.

First, there has been the influence of the Ecumenical Movement. For the first time for four hundred years, leaders of the largest and strongest churches (besides some of the smaller ones) have felt the need to heal their differences instead of perpetuating them. The World Missionary Conference of 1910 and the formation of the World Council of Churches in 1948 have been but landmarks in a process which initially involved Protestant churches, came to include the Orthodox churches and, since the Second Vatican Council of 1970, has embraced the Roman Catholic Church as well. In their search for unity, members

[1] C. H. Spurgeon, *Metropolitan Tabernacle Pulpit*, 1864, (Alabaster & Passmore, 1894; Pilgrim Publications, 1969) p. 328.

of WCC study groups have been forced to examine their own positions anew and to look with tolerance instead of hostility at the positions of others. At the same time the 'biblical theology' movement in the universities has forced all Christians (whatever their theological persuasion) to look again at the Scriptures and their meaning for the modern world, with many beneficial results.

While evangelical Christians have tended to be suspicious of the Ecumenical Movement itself, among themselves they have been unable to resist ecumenical pressures. The growth of the Scripture Union with its provision of Bible-reading and Sunday School teaching materials for all Christians regardless of denominational labels, the Keswick Convention with its motto *All One in Christ Jesus*, the rise of the Inter-Varsity Fellowship with its fast-growing Christian Unions in colleges and universities, the unity in evangelism experienced, particularly since 1950, in evangelistic campaigns large and small, have all brought evangelical Christians together as never before. Although baptism has usually been a taboo subject (for one must not rock the evangelical boat!), discussion, from time to time, has been inevitable. In many respects the evangelical developments of the twentieth century have been more impressive than the Ecumenical Movement, for the latter has been inspired by the leaders, while the former has been much more a grass-roots affair. Hence, in terms of the average Christian, it has been more real and relevant.

Secondly, the secularizing and de-christianizing effects of two world wars together with the rise of materialism have forced all Christians, in Western Europe at least, to re-examine their place in society. No longer can the leaders of the state churches maintain the fiction of a Christian country, no longer can they expect their pronouncements on ethical and social issues to be accepted as of right. Increasingly, in 'post-Christian' societies all Christians are reverting to the position of the early church, and the implications of this on their life and beliefs are immense. Paedobaptism is particularly involved. Indiscriminate baptism, as formerly practised, becomes ever more embarrassing, anachronistic and irrelevant. Adult baptism may come to involve the social isolation and possible persecution which is today the lot of believers in the Soviet Union and many other countries in the world.

A further problem arises from the present position of the Christian in a secular society. The stupidity, apart from the cost involved, of perpetuating denominational differences in new housing areas is leading increasingly to the creation in these areas of Christian centres, whose aim is to unite all Christians within one fellowship. As soon as this happens the practice of baptism becomes a key issue, and on the way it is resolved, the ecumenical character of the centre stands or falls. Thirdly, the mobility of modern society often makes baptism an intensely practical problem, particularly for the evangelical Christian. As he moves from school to college and on to a series of professional positions in different towns, or as unemployment in one area forces him to practise his trade in another, he is frequently faced with the prospect of changing his Christian fellowship. In these circumstances many find little attraction in holding, on principle, to their original denominational allegiance. They seek instead a church where the gospel is preached and the Bible is explained, regardless of the name on the board outside. Yet immediately, this presents them with problems. What should the crypto-Baptist do when children are born to him within the fellowship of an Anglican church? How should the crypto-Methodist who has baptized his children in infancy, advise his teenage sons and daughters when they come to apply for membership of a Baptist church? It is because these problems lead to the heart of the baptismal question that consideration must now be given to the practical issues which arise from the various practices of infant and adult baptism.

Part III

Baptism Today

11
Problems for paedobaptists

Between theory and practice there is often a great gulf fixed. It is one thing to make out a theoretical case for paedobaptism from the teaching of Scripture. It may be quite another to practise that baptism in the everyday life of the church, and remain true to the principles used in its justification. It is the authors' conviction that the way paedobaptism has been practised for centuries in both episcopal and non-episcopal churches, in both state and free churches, has resulted in much of the confusion surrounding its significance, and in most of the problems associated with its exercise at the present time. Some of these problems are administrative and peripheral only, and should be capable of fairly easy solution, while others are more serious and involve deep theological issues of their own.

Baptism in public or in private

Once the idea became current in the early church that infants should be baptized to cleanse them from original guilt inherited at birth, baptism *in extremis* became necessary. That is to say, if an infant looked like dying at birth (and before the age of scientific medicine there were many infants in this category) it must be baptized there and then, to save it from the flames of hell. Thus baptism in hospital, or at home, or anywhere where an unbaptized infant looked like passing from this world into the next, was allowed, as well as baptism in church. To the popular mind this gave the whole practice a superstitious rather than a theological significance. Baptism became not so much the way into the church as the way out of hell, and having the baby 'done' became all-important for reasons which many could not possibly explain. Furthermore, once baptism moved out of the church, its importance for the church inevitably declined. Church members could not possibly be expected to show true Christian concern for infants whose baptism they had not seen and might not even know about. From being a central rite of admission to the church, joyously witnessed by existing members of the church, baptism began its progress towards the side-lines and its scriptural meaning and importance began to be lost.

Baptism *in extremis* is rightly condemned by modern theologians. Thus Cullmann declares that as baptism signifies entry into the church on earth there is no need to baptize a dying infant as he will not enter the church on earth but will proceed straight to the church in heaven.[1] Nevertheless, old traditions die hard. Reports are still received of infants being baptized by nurses in hospital, while in the popular mind the compelling motive for baptism among parents who would otherwise rarely darken a church's door has changed little since the Middle Ages.

Closely akin to private baptism with all its unfortunate connotations is, in the authors' view, the much more widespread practice whereby many baptisms conducted in church are little more than private affairs for the families and friends of the infants concerned. In many episcopal churches baptismal services are usually held quite separately

[1] Cullmann, *Baptism in the New Testament* (English translation. SCM, 1950), p. 34, footnote 1.

from the main services of the week, while in non-episcopal churches baptisms are 'tacked on' to main services, the congregation being under no obligation to stay, and the parents, family and child attending for only the baptism. The frequent picture of proud parents, devoid of Christian understanding and making little effort to adhere to Christian moral and ethical standards in their private lives, bringing their new-born babies 'to be done' is no parody, but one repeated all too often in hundreds if not thousands of paedobaptist churches. Huddled around the font in a corner of an empty church, with father's courage suitably fortified in the public house, they hurry through a few words which mean nothing to them, listen to the assurance 'this child is regenerate', and return triumphantly homewards, the baby 'christened', the mother 'churched', the father relieved that the church roof did not fall in, the neighbours looking forward to eating the christening-cake and 'wetting the baby's head' with further supplies of beer.

How such a rite as this can be called *Christian* baptism by any standards is, in the authors' view, incomprehensible! If baptism is the means of entry into the church, then it should take place in the presence of the church congregation, not merely on church premises. If paedobaptism involves obligations for the church then as many church members as possible must attend baptisms that they might be aware of the obligations involved in receiving new members into the fellowship. If paedobaptism is to mean anything at all to those who are so baptized it must constantly be displayed before them, and its significance explained as they grow in the life of the church, but as long as baptism remains a hole-in-a-corner affair this can never be. As long as infant baptisms remain semi-private family occasions baptists will continue to point in contrast to their own celebrations of the rite when the whole congregation is present, when many remember their own baptism and renew their baptismal vows, when the gospel is proclaimed and when others are often converted by the public witness of the baptismal candidates.

Eligibility for paedobaptism

Reference was made earlier to differences of opinion among paedobaptists on this issue. Some advocate the baptism of as many infants as possible, others urge baptism whenever it is requested, while others contend that baptism should be administered only to the children of obviously Christian parents. It is the authors' conviction that a scriptural case can be made out for the last-named position only, and they share the view of many paedobaptists who argue that much of the scandal caused to baptists by paedobaptism is the result of the widespread indiscriminate administration of the rite. To say, however, that baptism is only for the children of Christian parents immediately creates a whole series of practical problems.

Firstly, there is the natural problem that Christian ministers find it hard to refuse requests for Christian services even to those who are not regular attenders at their churches. After all, they reason to themselves when confronted with a request for baptism from doubtful parents, might not the baptismal service itself kindle a spark of interest which, with careful, prayerful follow-up, will one day be fanned into a flame? Cannot the church fulfil its obligations to the baptized child through its prayers and Sunday School instruction, even if the parents and sponsors fail in theirs, and might not the sowing of the seed in this way one day bring forth good fruit? Added to this are the problems of unpopularity and misunderstanding when baptisms are refused. And in a day when church discipline of all kinds is notoriously lax, what point is there in refusing baptism in one church when parents determined 'to have the baby done' can have it baptized in another?

Secondly, even when a minister has decided to restrict

baptism to the children of Christian parents how does he decide which parents are Christians? Do parents who come to the major festivals and take the church magazine qualify? Should regular attendance Sunday by Sunday be necessary, or should baptism be restricted to the children of parents who come week by week to the communion table? An affirmative answer to any of these questions still does not solve the problem. Evangelicals are particularly aware of church members, regular in attendance at services, upright in character and conscientious in duty, who are still not Christians in the true sense of the word because they have never enjoyed a personal experience of Jesus Christ. Bold would be the minister indeed who would dare to refuse baptism to the children of such as these!

To the problem of which infants are eligible for baptism there is no final solution. Colin Buchanan's suggestion that 'the parents are to be living members of the church by communion if the children are to be newborn members of the church by baptism'[1] has much to commend it if only for its corollary that 'communion must take its rightful place in the life of the church'[2] and become 'the central service of the Sunday'.[3] Once communion ceases to be an optional extra service for the devout, held at a ridiculously early hour, or tacked on to a main service for those who wish to stay behind, churches will find it so much easier to define Christians and to distinguish them from adherents or enquirers. And in consequence, paedobaptismal discipline will become that much easier to exercise.

Baptism and confirmation

'If it is proper to administer baptism to infants,' declares John Murray, 'then the import of baptism must be the

[1] Buchanan, *Baptismal discipline* (Grove Books, 1972), p. 17.
[2] *Ibid.*
[3] *Ibid.*

same for infants as for adults. It cannot have one meaning for infants and another for adults.'[1] Quite so! Yet the failure to accept this conclusion in practical terms has created a situation where there are virtually two baptisms. Indeed, the Baptist theologian G. R. Beasley-Murray has pleaded powerfully for a recognition of this fact as a first step towards the solution of the baptismal controversy.[2]

For centuries the Western church has required those it has baptized as infants to submit to a further rite later in life called confirmation before admitting them to communion and full church membership. The development of confirmation and the fresh significance given to it by the Reformers have already been outlined.[3] In some episcopal churches it has the status of a sacrament and is strongly linked with the gift of the Holy Spirit. It is retained in various forms and in various names in non-episcopal churches which have continued to practise paedobaptism. Because it admits the candidate to full church membership there is an ever-present tendency for it to assume greater importance than baptism itself; indeed, at times, baptism has been seen as little more than a preparation for confirmation.

Twentieth-century Anglo-Catholic writers like Dix and Thornton have been persuasive exponents of the view that confirmation is taught in the New Testament and was always practised in the apostolic church.

From verses like 1 Corinthians 12:13 ('For by one Spirit we were all baptized into one body . . . and all were made to drink of one Spirit') and Galatians 4:6 ('And because you are sons, God has sent the Spirit of his Son into our hearts, crying "Abba! Father!" ') Thornton has detected

[1] Murray, *Christian baptism* (Presbyterian & Reformed Publishing Co., 1962), p. 48.

[2] Beasley-Murray, *Baptism today and tomorrow*, ch. 5.

[3] See above, p. 84f.

a distinction between baptism in water, whereby we become sons of God, and baptism in the Spirit, whereby our sonship is confirmed. This distinction, he contends, is given practical expression in the account of the conversion of the Samaritans in Acts 8 who, it will be recalled, were first baptized in water when they believed, and then were confirmed and received the Holy Spirit with the laying-on-of-hands by Peter and John. Thornton finds further support for his position in the distinction drawn by the writer to the Hebrews between 'ablutions' (*i.e.* baptism) and 'the laying on of hands' (6:2) (*i.e.* confirmation) and by the significance attached to the anointing of the Spirit (again understood as confirmation) in 1 John 2:20–27.[1]

Dix finds further support for his view that confirmation was practised in the apostolic church from his examination of the baptismal rite as described in the *Apostolic tradition* of Hippolytus. Hippolytus, it will be recalled, wrote in Rome at the turn of the second and third centuries and described a complex initiation rite which included anointing and laying-on-of-hands besides immersion in water. Here is clear evidence for Dix that the early church recognized a clear distinction between salvation (as signified by immersion) and the reception of the Spirit (signified by anointing and laying-on-of-hands). The two elements were normally celebrated together but could take place quite separately as the Samaritan example shows.

Fundamental to Dix's position is his assertion that the *Apostolic tradition* of Hippolytus is not merely descriptive of baptismal practice in Rome at the end of the second century, but, as its name implies, reflects the practice of the apostles themselves. Liturgy changes slowly, Dix contends, and Hippolytus was thus not describing new developments but long-established customs amply demonstrating that the apostles recognized the difference between

[1] Thornton, *Confirmation: Its place in the baptismal mystery*, (Dacre Press: A. & C. Black, 1954), *passim.*

baptism and confirmation and embodied it in their services in the church.[1]

So runs the argument, and as an explanation of how confirmation began to develop it is probably correct. Whether the theology behind it is equally correct is another matter. It is seriously questioned by other Anglican scholars. Writing, in 1927, of the distinction between water baptism and Spirit baptism, O. C. Quick declared, 'a theory which declares that Confirmation marks the first gift of the indwelling Spirit, and a practice which places Confirmation a dozen years or more after Baptism, point, when taken together, to conclusions which are intolerable'.[2] Later, in 1951, G. W. H. Lampe insisted that Dix had placed too much importance on Hippolytus and further denied that confirmation was to be found in the New Testament.[3] He tended to support the traditional evangelical view that once paedobaptism had become established confirmation was necessary to mark conversion and thus entry into full membership of the church.

The controversy has raged unabated for years, with a majority now appearing to be against the Thornton and Dix approach. In 1971 the Ely Report concluded that, baptism is the one rite of initiation into the Christian Church.[4] It went on to recommend radical alterations in the service of confirmation which would remove the idea that it marked the reception of the Holy Spirit in the baptized.

The radical approach of the Ely Report to the problems presented by confirmation enjoys the support of some evangelical Anglican writers. They have contended that if paedobaptism is true baptism it must indeed have the same

[1] Dix, *The theology of confirmation in relation to baptism*, *passim*.

[2] Quick, *The Christian sacraments* (Nesbitt, 1927), p. 184.

[3] Lampe, *The seal of the Spirit*, ch. 5.

[4] *Christian initiation, birth and growth in the Christian society* (CIO, 1971), ch. 4.

meaning for infants as for adults. Confirmation is thus an unscriptural and irrelevant appendage and must go, to be replaced perhaps by an annual service of ratification of baptismal vows attended by all baptized adults, at which members reaching the age of eighteen would be admitted to the electoral rolls of their churches. At the same time they recommend that baptized infants and children should be admitted to Holy Communion along with their parents, for their baptism, by its very nature, has qualified them for this.[1] In this connection several leading evangelical Anglicans are looking approvingly on the growing practice of Family Communion in the Church of England where children are encouraged to be present and to receive a blessing at the communion rail although as yet not partaking of the elements, and at the practice of the Eastern Orthodox churches where baptized infants and children receive communion regularly even while still babes in arms.

This is an admirably fresh and honest approach, but there are some telling objections to it. First, as Calvin long ago pointed out, communion is not a sacrament for infants. Those who partake are required to examine themselves beforehand (1 Cor. 11:28) and this, little children are incapable of doing.[2] Secondly, the advocates of infant and child communion seem to have forgotten that the Orthodox churches which they admire so warmly, administer communion to children because they have an *ex opere operato* view of its efficacy. That is to say, they believe that just as baptism brings its benefits automatically in the very act of being administered, so communion brings its benefits automatically and does not need to be received in faith by those who partake. Of course, the evangelicals would deny such conclusions, but we cannot but wonder, if infant and child communion became normal in paedo-

[1] Byworth, *Communion, confirmation and commitment* (Grove Books, 1972), *passim*.

[2] Calvin, *Institutes*, IV.xvi.30.

baptist churches; whether an *ex opere operato* view of communion among ordinary folk could be resisted. Is this the end of the road at which the evangelicals wish to arrive?

Thirdly, it would thus seem that the widespread adoption of infant and child communion and the abolition of confirmation would lead to the end of evangelical Christians as distinct groups within the major paedobaptist Protestant denominations. If truth were thereby vindicated that would be no tragedy. But would it? For if baptized children were brought up to believe that, by virtue of their baptism, they were Christians in the full sense of the word, and if they were strengthened in that belief week by week in partaking of Holy Communion, who would ever be able to persuade them of their need of a personal experience of Christ *for salvation*, for it is the insistence on the necessity of such an experience which is the hall-mark of the evangelical? Are the discoveries of Wesley and Whitefield and the tradition of Simeon, Ryle and Moule to be so lightly cast aside for the sake of theological consistency?

In all of these discussions one implication is difficult to avoid. The need for confirmation, felt by the overwhelming majority of paedobaptists for centuries, betrays the fundamental weakness in the paedobaptist case. Despite Murray's assertion at the head of this section (p. 157), 'the Baptism of Infants . . . cannot bear the whole weight of theological meaning which the New Testament places upon the Initiation of adults,'[1] and by their demand for confirmation most paedobaptists have been willing to admit this.

This leads really to the crux of the problem. What is the status of the baptized child in the eyes of God? Even Jesus needed to increase in wisdom and in stature, and in favour with God and man (Lk. 2:52). At the very least the baptized infant will need to follow his example, and some-

[1] *The theology of Christian initiation*, p. 12.

where along the line will need to make a personal ratification of his baptism in a personal acceptance of Jesus Christ as his Saviour and Lord. John Baillie has grappled brilliantly and lucidly with this problem in *Baptism and conversion.* He finds the solution in the distinction drawn in Reformed theology between regeneration and conversion. Regeneration is God's act of salvation by grace. Conversion, and that may be sudden and dramatic, or gradual and quiet, is man's response. At baptism an infant is made regenerate, but later in life he will still need to be converted. This too is a view that has its own problems. How these were raised at the time of the Wesleyan Revival has already been shown. But at least Baillie's conclusions do not lead to the wholesale abandonment of evangelical Christianity implicit in the abolition of confirmation and the admission of little children to communion, and there, for the time being, the issue must lie.

12
Problems for baptists

Defining the practices of those who baptize only adults is well-nigh impossible. There are so many different groups which do it. To begin with there are the self-confessed Baptist denominations. Loosely affiliated in the Baptist World Alliance, they could lay claim to being the largest non-national Protestant church in the world. In fact, they decline to use the word 'church' in this denominational sense, since most of the Baptist 'unions' or 'conventions' which are united in the Alliance are simply fellowships of independent congregations embracing a considerable variety of beliefs and practices. Sometimes this variety is so wide as to create suspicion and even scorn between various groups. This is particularly true where differences in American and English practice are concerned. All, however, insist that baptism must follow faith.

In addition to Baptists are the massive and multi-coloured Pentecostal traditions, the Brethren movement in several of its branches and the great majority of free evangelical churches. Overseas, many of the interdenominational 'faith' missionary societies have established indigenous churches in many countries with baptist theology. Finally there is the complex fact of the emergence of even more completely indigenous movements in Africa and Asia, totally independent of Western missionaries, largely uninterested in the history of Christendom, and usually carrying a strongly 'prophetic' or 'ecstatic' flavour. These, too, very often reject paedobaptism. Generalizations, therefore, form the stuff of this chapter, and apologies are offered in advance to any who feel that their particular insights have been ignored or misrepresented.

Fundamental to the position examined in this chapter and previously expounded, is the assertion that, in the New Testament, baptism is so inseparably linked to conscious faith that paedobaptism must be condemned as non-baptism. Infants are incapable of faith, therefore baptism cannot validly be applied to them. A necessary corollary to this position is the insistence that only in Baptist churches is true New Testament baptism preserved. Yet, in recent years, it is precisely this insistence which has come under increasing attack. Nor has the questioning come entirely from supporters of paedobaptism. The question being posed by some from both sides is this: can the modern practice of adult baptism really be equated with believers' baptism as practised in the New Testament?

Baptism and church membership

Baptism, it has been seen, was the means of entry into the New Testament church. In consequence, there are many churches where baptism is demanded as a precondition for membership. This means that people baptized in infancy and subsequently wishing to join a church in which perhaps they have been converted or spiritually helped must (by implication at least) renounce their former baptism and be rebaptized. Not surprisingly, this has caused a great deal of bitterness and recrimination. A convert may well find himself feeling like a shuttlecock as he bounds and rebounds between two indignant clergymen, both of whose judgments he respects. They are making demands on him which are mutually contradictory.

On the other hand, many English Baptist churches practising only adult baptism will admit a convert or more experienced Christian into membership simply 'on confession of faith'. The issue of baptism and rebaptism is judged by them to be a personal one to be decided by the conscience and conviction of each Christian. In such churches, the peculiar paradox may arise that, although they may be called Baptist churches, they rarely administer baptism, or administer it in complete separation from church membership. Even more oddly, it is perfectly possible to be a 'Baptist' without receiving any form of baptism at all, by any mode, either in infancy or in more mature years. A further curiosity is provided by those churches which practise only adult baptism and normally insist on it as a requirement for membership, unless some circumstance makes complete immersion difficult (as for example with a frail or crippled person). These churches then prefer a 'confession of faith' without baptism to the use of sprinkling or pouring. This suggests the extraordinary idea that the amount of water used is the most important feature in baptism. If there cannot be immersion, then regardless of the presence of water, the expression of faith, and the utterance of the triune Name, let there be no baptism at all – we shall be content to do without!

This loose approach to baptism and church membership is peculiarly English and is disowned by Baptists in virtually every other country, where baptism is regarded as an essential prerequisite for church membership. None the less it is worth asking how it has arisen.

In the past, two influences caused English Baptists to admit members without baptism. One was theological, the other practical. Theologically and historically, as explained in chapter 1, baptists have tended to view baptism as a symbolic ordinance and not as a sacrament. Being merely a symbol of faith and not a means of grace, baptism thus became less important than faith itself. It was faith which saved and faith which therefore became the true qualification for church membership. In consequence baptism was only of secondary importance and could, thus, be dispensed with altogether.

With this development went a recognition by English Baptists that others who did not share their views on baptism were none the less true Christians. If such, for various reasons, should wish to join baptist churches, their understandable reluctance to submit to rebaptism should not thereby disqualify them. They should be admitted on affirmation of faith.

Of these two developments the first is condemned by Beasley-Murray and the second praised.[1] To admit to full membership of a baptist church those in full membership of other churches without demanding adult baptism is, in his view, an act of Christian charity which some of those other churches could do well to emulate in return. But to admit to membership without baptism those from outside the Christian community altogether, or those who have grown up within the baptist church is quite alien to the teaching of the New Testament and should cease. Baptists can hardly expect paedobaptists to take them seriously when baptism is so lightly regarded among them.

Baptism and conversion

A more serious shortcoming in the way baptists practise baptism lies in its relation to conversion. In the New Testament baptism is always administered simultaneously with conversion or nearly so. Thus Peter's command on the Day of Pentecost was, ' "Repent, and be baptized ... for the forgiveness of your sins. . . ." So those who received his word were baptized, and there were added that day about three thousand souls' (Acts 2:38, 41). When the Samaritans believed Philip as he preached good news

[1] Beasley-Murray, *Baptism today and tomorrow*, pp. 86–88.

about the kingdom of God and the name of Jesus Christ, they were baptized, both men and women (Acts 8:12). When Ananias laid hands on Saul that he might regain his sight and be filled with the Holy Spirit, Saul rose and was baptized (see Acts 9:17, 18). As soon as Peter realized that the gift of the Holy Spirit had been poured out even on the Gentiles he commanded them to be baptized in the name of Jesus Christ (see Acts 10:45–48). When the Philippian gaoler and his household responded to Paul's and Silas' command to believe in the Lord Jesus he was baptized *at once*, with all his family (see Acts 16:30–33).

As was shown in chapter 1, baptism in the New Testament was part of the obedience of faith. Faith demanded action, immediate action, and that action was baptism. The idea of an unbaptized Christian is quite alien to the thought of the New Testament writers. Yet among modern baptists this understanding of the coincidence of baptism and faith has undergone considerable transition, to say the least. Baptism and conversion rarely, if ever, coincide, and may be separated by a period of months, or even years. In the process, baptism becomes something rather different from what it is in the New Testament.

Among modern baptists baptism is variously regarded. Sometimes it is understood as a step of personal obedience following the example of Jesus himself. Yet, as has been seen, in his baptism Jesus was not setting Christians an example but taking his place alongside sinful men and women 'to fulfil all righteousness' (Mt. 3:15). Sometimes baptism is understood as a witness to believers and unbelievers alike to a personal faith in Christ already existing and well established. Yet public baptism, in this sense, is not invariably required in the New Testament, otherwise Philip would not have baptized the Ethiopian eunuch on the edge of the Sinai desert and Paul would not have baptized the Philippian gaoler and his family in their own home in the middle of the night!

At other times baptists baptize as a reward for perseverance in faith. Baptism itself follows some time after conversion and is almost invariably preceded by a series of 'preparation classes' conducted by the minister. Measured by the example of the New Testament here is strange practice indeed! No suggestion can be found of Peter or Philip, Ananias or Paul holding baptismal preparation classes for their converts. Indeed circumstances surrounding the faith and baptism of their converts deny their possibility.

Another peculiar aspect of many modern adult baptisms is the frequent inclusion of the phrase addressed by the minister to the candidate immediately prior to the actual baptism itself: 'at your own request'. This too can find no support from the New Testament. Peter did not baptize Cornelius and his relatives and friends at their own request. 'He commanded them to be baptized' (Acts 10:48). Baptism for these was no optional extra preceded by self-examination to see if they were 'ready for baptism', it was a fundamental part of their coming to Christ and reception of the Holy Spirit. Once that had happened baptism had to follow.

Those who adopt these practices are, of course, quick to justify them. In protest against what they see as the compulsory baptism of infants who cannot make a choice, they feel it right that the impetus for baptism should come from the candidate. They wish to avoid any sense of coercion. Hence the formula, 'at your own request'. As far as prolonged preparation is concerned, they point to the undoubted fact that many people influenced by campaigns, special efforts and the regular witness of the church, make an initial response to the gospel only to fall away later and abandon the Christian life. Baptism is a solemn ordinance, and they feel that the candidate should prove himself and should have more knowledge of the faith he claims to be embracing.

This kind of thinking, sensible and cautious though it is, really evades the central issue. Is baptism as we have just described it the baptism of the New Testament? Or is it not more like the kind of post-apostolic development described in chapter 4? Fundamental to the baptist case is the assertion that paedobaptism is not the baptism of the New Testament. Beasley-Murray, for example, quotes with approval the judgment of the French Reformed theologian F. J. Leenhardt concerning paedobaptism: 'Truly, a new sacrament has been invented!'[1] Yet can he be so certain that adult baptism as administered in many churches today is not open to very nearly the same charge?

Of course the people mentioned in Acts (the Pentecostal converts, the Samaritan believers, Lydia, the Philippian gaoler and the rest) were baptized because they wished to be, and therefore 'at their own request'. But then they were professing conversion at the time. Is this really the same as mature Christians 'requesting' to be baptized because the church they admire enjoins it, or because they wish to protest against an earlier mode of baptism which they have come to reject?

Naturally, too, baptist ministers want to avoid baptizing people who might later fall away, but was not this problem shared by the apostles? Their letters provide ample evidence that indeed it was. The names of some of those who disappointed them are even recorded (see *e.g.* 1 Tim. 1:19, 20; 2 Tim. 4:10)! Acts itself tells of Simon the magician who made some kind of profession of faith, was baptized, and then revealed how little he was inwardly changed (Acts 8:9–23). Nevertheless, the apostles preached baptism in the same breath as repentance, and previous disappointments seem not to have discouraged them from baptizing converts immediately, as part of their conversion and initiation experience. When their converts did fall away, or were in danger of growing slack and

[1] Beasley-Murray, *Baptism today and tomorrow*, p. 157.

careless, it was to their baptism and its significance that the apostles sometimes appealed in seeking to restore or warn them: 'How can we who died to sin still live in it? Do you not know that all of us who have been baptized into Christ Jesus were baptized into his death? We were buried therefore with him by baptism into death, so that as Christ was raised from the dead by the glory of the Father, we too might walk in newness of life' (Rom. 6:2–4). 'For as many of you as were baptized into Christ have put on Christ' (Gal. 3:27).

Now, if New Testament baptism is conversion-baptism, is the immersion of a believer taking a step of obedience, making a public witness or graduating from a course of instruction, the same thing? The acceptance of a course of teaching or the completion of a period of probation are obviously praiseworthy things, but do they constitute the conditions of New Testament baptism? The decision to reject a state church system, or the decision to join the local Baptist church may be choices carefully and sincerely made, but do they fulfil the requirements of New Testament baptism? Or could it be that another 'new sacrament' has been invented?

One obvious conclusion may be reached from a consideration of these difficulties. It is that the kind of practice just described argues not so much for New Testament baptism as for a New Testament church. Many baptists would agree with this assertion. Their position results from their determination to preserve local churches as communities of believers. The church is made up of Christians and only Christians. One becomes a Christian by personal faith in Christ, and proves it by a changed life. Therefore infants cannot be Christians, should not be regarded as church members and should not receive the church ordinance of baptism. On the contrary, adult folk able to make a meaningful choice, should be urged to put their confidence in Christ, should then receive a course of instruction and, having proved as far as possible the reality of their faith, should be incorporated by baptism into a community of similarly committed Christians.

No-one would wish to decry such a vision. Earlier chapters have shown how it is one which has haunted the imagination and stirred the hopes of successive generations of Christians. Yet the paedobaptist would wish to assert that in practice it is unrealistic, and to ask whether something unrealistic can really be scriptural. The plain fact is that the most careful probationary period and preparation classes cannot ensure either that only true believers will be baptized and join the church, or that genuine believers who do this will not later make mistakes which gravely compromise their testimony and that of the church. Did not Jesus himself teach that, like the seed which fell on rocky ground and among thorns, some people would apparently receive the word, only to reject it later (Mt. 13:20–22)? Did he not also warn that Christians and non-Christians would be mixed inextricably together like wheat and weeds (Mt. 13:24–30)? And did not Paul describe how God was displeased with most of those who were baptized into Moses, without any suggestion that their baptism was in any way irregular (see 1 Cor. 10:1–5)?

Here is a hard issue indeed and one which most certainly lies at the root of the baptismal controversy. Here is one reason why that controversy is so intractable, and because it is so intractable, here is a call for understanding and tolerance and charity from all involved, those who feel so passionately for the purity of the church on earth, and those content to await that perfect purity in heaven.

Baptism and children

If baptists find difficulty in administering baptism at the time of conversion, they face even greater problems in applying New Testament principles where the conversion of children is involved. As has been already stated baptists in Britain today are usually unwilling to baptize children much under the age of fourteen, yet the theological implications of this position are far-reaching indeed and difficult to reconcile with the teaching of the New Testament.

If baptism is to be administered at the time of conversion and if baptists refuse to baptize children younger than fourteen (or thirteen, or twelve, or whatever) then they are implying that all such children cannot be converted and must, therefore, for the sake of consistency, be treated as outsiders. Initially, of course, the question is raised, at what age can a child consciously believe? Little children of three and four are often far more conscious of the reality and nearness of Christ than their parents; should they be baptized? Baptists, as was seen earlier, are willing enough to allow that Polycarp was baptized as a child in AD 70: why then do they refuse such baptism to their own children? Could it be that a serious attempt by baptists to baptize on conversion according to the New Testament pattern, would lead them inexorably, and perhaps very rapidly, towards a position of child baptism, little different from infant baptism? The conclusion seems inescapable. Why then do baptists shrink from such a conclusion? Because their children might later repudiate their baptism on growing up? But then, many who are baptized as adults repudiate their baptism in later years. Would child baptism, with all the uncertainties involved, compromise the baptist attempt to build a pure church? Perhaps so, and perhaps this is the real reason why baptism is denied to children.

Apart from the inconsistency of refusing baptism to an obviously Christian child, such a refusal could have a harmful effect on the child's whole development. To refuse baptism is to deny the presence of Christian faith. How insecure will such a child then feel, having sincerely repented of wrong-doing and invited the Saviour into his life, only to find that that, apparently, is still not enough!

In addition to all this is the sheer impossibility of treating children as strangers to God's grace. What baptist parent does not teach his child to pray from his earliest years? What Christian parent does not instruct his children in right and wrong from the standards of Scripture? What such parent does not take his children to church to share in the worship of the believing community? And what parent does not believe that God hears his children's prayers and accepts the worship of their hearts, and does not teach them so? Yet if such children belong to Christ should they not be baptized, for is not baptism baptism into Christ? If the wives, husbands and slaves at Ephesus and Colossae to whom Paul wrote were baptized, can the baptist be so certain that the children simultaneously addressed were not similarly baptized (see Eph. 5:21–6:9; Col. 3:18–25)? Can it seriously be entertained that the 'little children' to whom John wrote because their sins were forgiven had not enjoyed tangible evidence of that forgiveness in the waters of baptism (see 1 Jn. 2:12)?

American Baptists, on reading these paragraphs, might well be forgiven for smiling unsympathetically at the problems their English brethren have created for themselves by their refusal to baptize much before the age of fourteen. In baptizing their own children at around seven years of age, immediately after their first profession of faith with no probation period between, they obviously avoid many of the problems outlined above. None the less, the English situation shows how, even among baptists, baptismal practice is often as much the result of tradition as is the practice of those they oppose so fiercely. Recognition of this might, one hopes, induce a greater spirit of humility among them and a fresh willingness to re-examine their own traditions in the light of New Testament teaching.

Baptism and dedication

If baptists face problems in relating their practice to the New Testament in matters of church membership, conversion and their attitude to children, they face even greater problems in their approach to infants. Most baptist churches, whatever their denominational allegiance, hold services of thanksgiving and dedication on the birth of a child. These services are usually included in the main Sunday service of worship, either as an integral part of that service, or added on at the end with the congregation remaining. Although held usually for the newly-born children of church members, many churches will conduct these services for any parents who ask for them.

At dedication services God is given thanks for the safe delivery of the child, the parents promise to bring up the child in the Christian faith, he is named and 'dedicated', that is to say, the pious hope is expressed that in due time he will come to a personal faith in Christ, and prayers are offered for parents and child in their family life together. In many respects the language used in some dedication services is similar to that used in infant baptismal services, and while water, of course, is not used, the minister usually lays his hands on the head of the infant at the moment of dedication. Among modern baptists dedication services became popular only during the nineteenth century and then only amid some controversy, although, as was shown earlier, something similar to dedication services had a long and honoured history among the Paulicians of the Middle Ages and before.

Surprisingly, leading contemporary baptist theologians seem little concerned with the theology and implications of dedication, apparently taking it for granted as a natural and proper way of marking the birth of children to Christian parents, yet its implications are immense, and if thought through, might be seen to compromise the whole baptist position.

Of recent years Neville Clark has been almost alone in attempting a serious theological justification of the practice,[1] and his distinction between 'believers (and their children)' and 'unbelievers (and their children)' smacks of some arguments in favour of infant *baptism* rather than dedication. Indeed, paedobaptists reading Clark will be puzzled and mystified as to why his distinction leads him to urge only dedication and not baptism for the children of believers. Perhaps significantly, Clark's views have found little acceptance among baptists in general who, when pressed, tend to justify dedication in a variety of other ways.

Some, for instance, appeal to the example of Hannah who lent Samuel to the LORD as long as he lived, in gratitude to God for answering her prayer for a child (see 1 Sa. 1 and 2, especially 1:11, 22, 28). In her willingness to place Samuel in God's service Hannah is regarded as an example to all Christian parents who should similarly be selfless towards their own children, not wanting them for themselves, but for Christ, in salvation and service.

Hannah's selfless giving of Samuel back to the God who gave him in the first place is indeed a fine example to all godly parents, but that hardly justifies exalting her action into a rite to be observed by contemporary Christians. For a start Hannah's action, although exemplary, was clearly exceptional and was recorded for that reason. Had God intended it to be copied by Christian parents, surely it would have been copied by Jewish parents first, and there would have been some scriptural record of this.

Secondly, Hannah's dedication of Samuel (if so it can be called) was not a dedication for salvation but for service. While service may be explicit in a modern dedication,

[1] Clark, *The theology of baptism*, in Gilmore (Ed.), *Christian baptism* (Lutterworth, 1970), pp. 320–326.

salvation is what is really in mind. When Samuel was returned to the Temple to Eli he was already 'saved' in the sense that, like all Jewish boys, he belonged to the covenant people of God by circumcision. Within that relationship Hannah wished him to progress as far as he could in God's service.

Thirdly, when Samuel was 'dedicated' he was not an infant but a weaned child (see 1 Sa. 1:22–24) and as weaning then took place at a later age than it does today he may have been between six and ten years of age. Fourthly, if Hannah is to be an example to Christian parents, they must baptize their children, for, as suggested already, Samuel would have been circumcised when eight days old, and that, for Hannah, would no doubt have been her first step in giving him back to God. Hannah's example will simply not fit into baptist theology, for once it is granted that the Old Testament justifies Christian practice in one respect, then that Testament must justify practice in other respects too, namely paedobaptism. Yet, as has been demonstrated already, many baptists deny paedobaptism on the grounds of the discontinuity of the Old and New Testaments.

Other baptists appeal to the account of the presentation of Jesus in the Temple to justify infant dedication (see Lk. 2:22–40). As Mary and Joseph took the infant Jesus to the Temple and offered sacrifices to God, so Christian parents should take their infant children to church to offer sacrifices of praise and thanksgiving for their birth.

This line of reasoning, however, suffers from all the defects of the first, about Hannah and Samuel. Jesus' presentation in the Temple was a Jewish ritual, not of thanksgiving, but of purification, and Mary was its real subject, not Jesus (see Lv. 12:6–8). Its only modern counterpart is perhaps the Churching of Women and baptists would eschew that more fiercely than paedobaptism! What is more to the point is that before Jesus was presented he was circumcised (see Lk. 2:21), and if he is therefore to be an example to the children of Christian parents then they should be baptized rather than dedicated!

Yet other baptists justify dedication from the Gospel accounts of Jesus blessing the children; indeed these accounts often feature in dedication services (see Mt. 19:13–15; Mk. 10:13–16; Lk. 18:15–17). The trouble with this approach is that all the arguments marshalled by baptists against using these verses to justify paedobaptism apply equally to dedication. It was *children* who were brought to Jesus, children old enough to come. Even if there were a few infants among them (see Lk. 18:15) it was of *children*, not infants, that Jesus said, 'To such belongs the kingdom of God' (Lk. 18:16). Baptists really cannot have their cake and eat it! If the Gospel incident has nothing to do with *infant* baptism, neither has it anything to do with *infant* dedication.

Baptists would wish to rebut this statement. They would point out that the example of Jesus does in fact underline a general principle that children are invited into the love and blessing of Christ. Dedication, they would contend, says that and no more: paedobaptism says much more, and says it mistakenly. The error of paedobaptism, they would argue, lies not in thinking that the gospel has something to say to parents and children, but in confusing what it says with baptism. Dedication says it eloquently, and without the fatal confusion. If it be objected that a general principle has been sharpened into a specific rite without actual biblical sanction, could not the same be said, asks the baptist, about church wedding-services or funerals?

Clearly, there is no purpose in simply trying to score points. The baptist is trying hard to say and do something which matters very much. The intriguing thing is that the paedobaptist is often trying to say and do the very same thing. Neither has a specific biblical command which can be quoted in support of his practice towards infants. Both would admit that the increased employment of their respective practices arose from popular demand and from the need to say something about the solidarity of the Christian family. Both *should* admit that the practice can and does degenerate into an indiscriminate acceptance of 'having the baby done' – a folk-custom and a sociological phenomenon. And the baptist should learn to be a little less scornful of his paedobaptist brother for adopting a custom that has no clear scriptural precedent – neither has his own!

Really, however, the issue goes deeper than this. For, as confirmation was seen to compromise the paedobaptist position, so dedication compromises the baptist position. As the paedobaptist finds that paedobaptism does not tell the whole story and needs to be supplemented by confirmation, so the baptist finds himself in a similar dilemma. For somewhere in his system the baptist has to find room for 1 Corinthians 7:14 ('your children . . . are holy'), and try as he will he cannot escape Kingdon's conclusion 'that, even where there is only one believing partner in a marriage, the children who are born are in a state of privilege'.[1] Precisely, says the paedobaptist, that is why we baptize them. No, retorts the baptist, 'being in a state of privilege does not furnish a proper ground for baptism'.[2] Maybe it doesn't, but where the children of Christians are concerned, believer's baptism, like paedobaptism, fails to tell the whole story. As confirmation has had to be invented in recognition of the response of faith, so dedication has had to be invented in recognition of the gracious love of God which extends to 'children and their children's children . . . for ever' (Ezk. 37:25).

[1] Kingdon, *Children of Abraham*, p. 90.
[2] *Ibid.*

13
The real issues

From Tertullian to Spurgeon, Christians have protested against paedobaptism and have been answered in kind by those with whom they have disagreed. Through the centuries many of the arguments have had a familiar ring, and although today controversy has been succeeded by dialogue, baptism is once again the subject of keen discussion among Christians of all kinds. This book has attempted to chart the main positions adopted on both sides in the past and in the present. Now it is time to draw the threads of the arguments together and ask why the water which should unite Christians in the Body of Christ continues to divide. There are perhaps six main issues on which the controversy turns. The positions Christians adopt on these issues will largely determine whether they will baptize their children or whether they will withhold that baptism until a conscious confession of faith is made.

1. The nature of baptismal grace

For our salvation we are dependent on the grace of God. On that, all Christians agree. But how and when and where is that grace applied? The extreme sacramentalist view links it with external religious rites (and especially with baptism) in an almost automatic manner which obscures the need for repentance and faith. Salvation is conveyed by the correct observation of the externals, the water and the triune Name. This is held to be sufficient, quite regardless of the state of mind and will of the candidate for baptism either at the time or subsequently. It is startling both in its exclusivism and in its inclusivism. It excludes from the kingdom of God all who have not received baptism, regardless of their faith; it counts as Christians all who have been baptized, regardless of their lack of faith.

At the other extreme are those who regard baptism as a mere external symbol. Since salvation can be received only by faith, no religious rite can be associated with it in such a way as to confuse that fact. Baptism may very well be received, but it is received only as an 'ordinance' and can, if necessary, be dispensed with altogether. Its only connection with grace is that it presents striking pictures and symbols of what grace imparts through faith.

Naturally enough, sacramentalists tend to be paedobaptists desirous of bringing salvation through baptism to all new-born children as soon as possible. Those who hold to a symbolic view of baptism tend to delay it until a conscious confession of faith is made.

Concerning the nature of baptismal grace we have urged a middle way. Baptism does not bring salvation automatically, by the work being worked, but neither is it merely symbolic. It is a sacrament which brings grace through faith. It is part of the obedience of faith. The act of baptism demonstrates that faith is active for salvation.

2. The nature of saving faith

Discussion about the relationship of faith and baptism to salvation leads to discussion about the nature of saving faith itself. 'By grace you have been saved through faith,' says Paul (Eph. 2:8); but must that faith always be exercised exclusively for one's own salvation, or may it sometimes be exercised for the salvation of another, particularly one's child? Those who answer according to the first alternative will restrict baptism to those who show that they have believed, while those who answer according to the second will be willing to baptize the children of believers as well.

3. The nature of salvation

It is one thing to define the extent of saving faith, but what of salvation itself? In what sense do we use the word, especially in the context of baptism? Are we thinking of its objective existence in the declared purpose of God, or its subjective existence in the declared experience of the believer? Is the key phrase, 'God has chosen to save me', or, 'I have chosen to be saved'?

Those who stress the objective aspects of salvation tend to be paedobaptists, seeing in paedobaptism the operation of the prevenient grace of God, while those who stress its subjective aspects tend to be baptists, seeing baptism as a demonstration of a salvation which has already been received. In this respect the baptismal controversy is part of the wider controversy between 'Calvinists' and 'Arminians', between 'Augustinians' and 'Pelagians', between those who contend for the sovereignty of God in all human affairs, and those who uphold the idea of human free will. This is not to say that many baptists are not Calvinists and many paedobaptists are not Arminians, but the baptismal controversy is most certainly a development of that deeper division of opinion.

Of course, it is correct to view salvation both objectively and subjectively. 'By grace you have been saved through faith; and this is not your own doing, it is the gift of God' (Eph. 2:8). It is right to emphasize that salvation is all of God and utterly dependent upon his grace, a grace that flowed freely towards men when there was nothing in them to merit his love, and no inclination in them to choose his ways. But it is equally important to emphasize the response from men which the gospel calls forth. The Bible assumes that Christians believe, know what they believe and rejoice in the consequences of believing. It is this dual aspect of salvation and its expression in baptism which tends to make the baptismal controversy so intractable.

4. The nature of the church on earth

Baptism is baptism into Christ and into his Body, the church. But what is the church, particularly as it exists on earth? Is it just the company of the faithful, or should it seek to draw as many as possible into its ranks and thereby bring them to saving faith in Christ? If the church is to be an exclusive body, limited to those with faith in Christ, then baptism must be an exclusive rite, administered only where faith is obviously present. If God alone knows the hearts of men, and if the church is therefore to be an inclusive body, then it will be easy to baptize infants and children that they might grow as members of the worshipping community and take their place among the followers of Christ.

5. The nature of the covenant of grace

Covenant theology takes a prominent place in the Scriptures. Is there one covenant underlying both Old and New Testaments, or is there fundamental contrast between two covenants? If there is one covenant, is it fair to assume that the initiatory rite of circumcision in the Old Testament has an exact correspondence with the initiatory rite of baptism in the New? Paedobaptists declare that a fundamental promise of grace is obscured if that is *not* assumed: namely the loving purpose of God for believers *and their children*. If it *is* assumed, warn baptists, an even more fundamental feature of the gospel is obscured: its demand for personal believing response.

The trouble unfortunately is that, whatever the exact relationship between circumcision and baptism may be, Scripture nowhere draws the explicit conclusions about paedobaptism, one way or the other, that have been outlined so far in this book. Is it not significant that both the baptist and paedobaptist positions rely heavily on the silence of Scripture? The absence of any specific infant baptism supposedly clinches the baptist's case: the failure of Scripture to record the baptism of an adult previously born to Christian parents proves the case the other way for the paedobaptist. Yet arguments from silence are notoriously suspect, and the fact that Christians need to appeal to silence to support their baptismal positions should make them cautious, to say the least, in forcing those conclusions on each other. It is because Scripture is silent that Christians can legitimately hold different views as to who should be baptized. They always have done, still do and probably always will. What is important is that those views should be held in love, understanding and humility, with a willingness to seek forgiveness for past sins, and a desire to let the water that divides divide no longer.

6. The status of the Christians' child

Carried to its logical extreme, paedobaptism teaches that every child who is baptized is safe for eternity just because he has been baptized. Yet, as has been shown, Protestant paedobaptists have rightly shrunk from this conclusion and have been glad to demand a response of faith from the growing child, and to recognize this in confirmation. Carried to its equally logical extreme the theology of believers' baptism denies any special status to the children of Christian parents, demanding that as they grow to discretion they must seek regeneration and salvation on the same terms as the children of unbelieving parents. Yet no baptist really believes this either. No baptist who loses an infant child believes that his child perishes in Hell because he has never repented of his sin and trusted in Christ for salvation. Such a bereaved parent looks to the mercy and grace of God and says with David, who also lost an infant child, 'I shall go to him, but he will not return to me' (2 Sa. 12:23). Why? Because his child is in a state of privilege. Instinctively, or through an honest appreciation of the clear teaching of Scripture, the baptist knows his child is privileged. He is privileged to be born into a Christian home and introduced early into the life of the Christian church. He is privileged because he is included in God's covenant in Christ on account of his parents' faith, and baptists are happy to recognize this in their rite of dedication.

To say that the child of Christian parents is privileged must not be misunderstood. It does not mean that he is unequivocally a Christian in the full New Testament sense. Nor does it mean that he will inevitably remain within the Christian fold. That would be to repeat the error of sacramentalism and to make being a Christian solely dependent on something external and mechanical, namely, birth into the right family. Nor does it absolve the child from the obligation to repent and believe. Indeed, because he has been born into the covenant people of God this obligation is all the more pronounced. All through his life he must repent and believe. Sometimes he will resist God's call. At other times the love and mercy of Christ will come to him in a new way and he will be able to look back on meaningful moments and periods in his Christian pilgrimage. Nor does the child's privileged status absolve his parents from responsibility for his spiritual condition. It is because their child is included in the covenant that they must instruct him in its terms and conditions, in other words, they must lead him to Christ. Sometimes they will rejoice at his response. At other times they will need to claim the covenant in prayer for their child as they see him sinful and wilful and resistant to the claims of God's love.

Bringing up a child in the discipline and instruction of the Lord is demanded of all Christian parents (see Eph. 6:4). Many will rejoice as their children confirm their call and election in personal faith and trust in the Lord Jesus Christ (see 2 Pet. 1:10). Others will weep when their children resolutely deny their Lord and Saviour and turn their backs with set purpose against the God who loves them and calls them. For surely it is no accident that the strongest warnings against apostasy in the whole of the New Testament come in the Letter to the Hebrews, written to Christians who were perhaps more conscious of their place in the covenant with God than most of their contemporaries. For God's love can be spurned, his mercy can be denied, and none perhaps fall farther from grace than those who turn their back on the loving influences of a Christian home.

All of this, of course, has little to do with baptism, and it is one of the tragedies of Christian history that many Christians have failed to recognize this. To insist that the inclusion of children in the people of God *must* be ratified in their baptism in infancy is to come dangerously close to sacramentalism and to making Christianity depend on external observance more than on inward faith, in this case the faith of the parents in the electing love of God towards their child. Equally to demand that baptism *must* await the personal response of faith in the child, with all the problems of deciding when that has taken place, is to deny to parents a great comfort, a visible sign that their children are his because they are his, that he will call them by grace, that they will trust Christ for salvation, that they will enjoy the hope of glory.

Christians must agree to differ at this point because Scripture gives them no specific instructions concerning their children. Paedobaptism and believers' baptism both testify to different aspects of God's dealings with men. Because they are applied to humans, both fall short of their intended purpose. Both can be dreadfully abused, yet Christians are commanded to baptize and to be baptized, and they must respect the varying ways they find God leading them to observe his commands.

14
Towards tomorrow

The urgent problem

The course of this book has taken some strange by-paths, and has raised some perplexing issues. Has the exercise been worth while? After all, the Christian church of the seventies has a good deal on its hands. Threatened by militant atheism, hammered by persecution, thwarted by indifference, should it not be concentrating on absolute essentials? And now that we are in the age of ecumenism, surely we can forget about trifles like baptism, can't we? Emphatically no!

As we saw earlier in the Introduction, it is precisely the present climate within our churches that often causes baptismal differences to become a practical problem: less interaction between denominations made it easier for people to ignore the whole issue, or to leave it in the realm of theory. Today, more than ever, we need to look closely at our baptismal beliefs and practices so that we know, first of all, what we believe and why; and secondly, why others differ from us. But the issues are not just academic: they affect the lives of ordinary Christians and can play a big part, positive or negative, in the church's witness.

One of the authors, with his wife, recently worshipped on holiday at a seaside parish church. The pews were well-filled, the atmosphere friendly, the liturgy was followed with reverence and joy, and the sermon preached in an attractive, persuasive and biblical manner. A service of infant baptism followed. The proud parents stood with twenty friends and relatives, obviously not used to church, but clearly impressed and interested. *Series Two* was followed loosely, with further adaptations by the vicar. The need for parents and child to turn to Christ was clearly underlined. Not a trace of magical virtue was attributed to the rite. A baptist could object to nothing except the use of water: what an Anglican with Catholic tendencies would have felt is difficult to imagine. Turning to greet several church members in their early twenties, we congratulated them on the form of the service. They happily replied, 'Yes, it's an improvement – but just wait until we get rid of infant baptism altogether!' To them, the issue was not academic, but scorchingly practical. They were posing the question, 'How can we make baptism an aid to evangelism and our expression of the gospel among our generation?'

A few weeks later the same writer visited new residents in his own town. Their regular attendance at church services had been noted and followed up. Father, mother, teenage son and teenage daughter greeted the minister with pleasure, and poured out their questions. Son had become a Christian at the school Christian Union, and was consequently confirmed at the village church, a ceremony full of meaning in the first flush of his new-found faith. Mother, baptized in a Congregational church as a baby, had been too busy to attend church ever since, it seemed. However, impressed by the change in her son, she had attended a pentecostal campaign in an Anglican church and had had a vital encounter with Christ. Father was a bit bewildered by all this, but had begun to attend our Free church. Nothing dramatic had happened. There was no date on which he could fix a sudden conversion, but he had found himself responding with increasing warmth and concern to the preaching. Daughter was at the end of the queue, interested, happy to attend, pleased to see many of her own age-group in church, willing to be instructed. Then came the questions.

Since the son's confirmation had come after his conversion and had, in his belief, 'made good' his infant baptism, could he be received into membership without being baptized again? Since the wife's infant baptism had meant nothing to her then or since, having now found Christ could she be baptized as a believer? Since the father was the head of the house, should the son's membership and the wife's baptism be delayed until the father could lead his whole family in an honest and assured confession of faith? And had the daughter enough conviction to join them? There, in a nutshell, was the kind of pastoral problem raised by the baptismal controversy. God was clearly at work in a whole family. Would the customs of the local church help or hinder that work? A purely academic argument? No, but a pressingly practical problem!

The Council of Jerusalem

What can be done about such situations? Can we find more in the Bible to guide us than further texts to hurl at one another across the baptismal divide? At the end of Paul's first missionary journey in Asia Minor, the Christian church was faced with a major crisis. An argument arose which involved practices fundamental to the nature of the gospel. In their confusion, Christians were 'scandalizing' each other by their actions. The point at issue was whether or not Gentile converts to Christianity should have to be circumcised and undertake to observe the whole ceremonial law of Moses before they were admitted to membership of the church. Converted Pharisees were demanding circumcision. Paul and his associates were strenuously denying its necessity. The Pharisees scandalized Paul by placing converts under a bondage to legal demands, thus obscuring the essentials of the gospel of grace. Gentile converts scandalized Jewish Christians by scant regard for some of the laws of Moses which affected everyday living and social intercourse. James's solution of the argument was remarkable for the way in which it safeguarded evangelical liberty while at the same time removing the causes of scandal between the two groups (see Acts 15:1–21).

In many respects the baptismal controversy resembles the old circumcision disagreement. At stake is both the essential nature of the gospel, and the tendency of Christians to grieve and offend each other by their diverse practices. Those who baptize infants scandalize their fellow Christians who feel that fundamental features of the gospel are being obscured. Those who baptize only believers scandalize their fellow Christians by denying and even deriding a practice whose supporters believe it dates from New Testament times and is commanded in Scripture itself. Can some kind of solution be found in the spirit of Acts 15?

In attempting to answer this question, it is instructive to notice first, how the apostles and disciples reached their point of agreement, and secondly, just what the agreement involved. To begin with, there was a full, frank and open discussion. The Christians 'gathered together to consider this matter' (verse 6) and there was 'much debate' (verse 7). This is striking when it is considered that the very men who had been called and taught by Jesus were there to give what could well have been an authoritative pronouncement at the very beginning. Had they done so, however, genuine fears, suspicions and misunderstandings would have remained beneath the surface. It was better to 'have it out'. The Greek word, *suzētēsis*, which is translated 'debate', implies seeking, questioning and searching, with an absence of entrenched positions and immovable convictions. If such an attitude was appropriate even in the presence of apostles, how much more is it desirable in any effort to resolve the baptismal problem, bedevilled as it is by centuries of tradition and dispute.

Following the discussion was a period of witness, when all were reminded of the experiences of both Peter and Paul. Peter recalled the dramatic incident at Caesarea when God gave his Spirit to uncircumcised Gentiles 'just as he did to us' (verse 8). Barnabas and Paul related the more recent triumphs of the Gentile mission and the signs and wonders God had done through them (verse 12). Thus the assembled disciples were given facts as well as ideas – and were willing to face the implication of these facts. God 'made no distinction between us and them, but cleansed their hearts by faith' (verse 9), 'giving them the Holy Spirit just as he did to us' (verse 8). That was the double lesson to be learnt: God was at work in sovereign power, giving his Spirit to people whose condition did not fit in with preconceived ideas, and the basis on which he worked was *grace received through faith*. The facts surprised many of the Jewish Christians, but the facts were plain and the lesson was duly learnt.

The application of this principle to the present baptismal controversy is obvious. God is manifestly at work by his Spirit on both sides of the baptismal divide. A thorough-going paedobaptist should not be surprised when the children of baptist parents who neither recognized nor gave symbolic expression to the 'covenant-promises' do as a matter of fact often turn to Christ in later years. Equally, a fervent baptist should not be surprised when the Holy Spirit continues to work in circles where (he feels) the need for personal decisive commitment is confused by a premature sacrament. Yet the facts proclaim that this is so.

As far as the United Kingdom is concerned it can be fairly said that the two major denominations most clearly committed to evangelistic activity are the Baptists and the Church of England. Yet they stand as far apart as any two Protestant movements could stand on the issue of baptism, without (apparently) their evangelism being compromised. The Holy Spirit is active in both communions, 'cleansing their hearts by faith'. Can this not be humbly and heartily recognized? And can a possible conclusion be drawn from the fact that the Holy Spirit, judging by his own activity, does not find the differences of judgment on baptism as great an obstacle as many of us do?

As Peter and Paul related their experiences, all the assembly kept silence and listened (verse 12). That is not easy when convictions are firmly held. It is easier to keep trying to make one's point, to leap in with a devastating reply, to drag the discussion back on to familiar lines laid out by preconceived ideas. Yet unless there is listening, there will never be understanding, and without understanding there can never be tolerance. By presenting conflicting views, as we have throughout this book, our aim as authors has been to make this listening and understanding process easier for all.

Throughout the debate, too, the apostles and disciples at Jerusalem kept one great principle in mind. It is the central truth which must be preserved in any discussion about baptism. 'We believe that we shall be saved through the grace of the Lord Jesus, just as they will' (verse 11). The centrality of grace is crucial. Whatever agreements and accommodations are made between Christians who differ in understanding, they must not cloud this issue. If the practice of baptism obscures the message of the willingness of God to forgive and renew those who do not deserve and cannot earn his favour, then that practice must be wrong. If differences of opinion about baptism lead different groups of Christians to deny acceptance with them of people who have been accepted by God, then Christians are being more particular than God himself. The apostles kept this principle clearly in mind, although they reached what was essentially a compromise solution. It was a solution which made concession to tradition and local feeling, but which clung firmly to the centrality of grace. When some of the stricter Jewish party later took advantage of this to push their demands further, Paul had no hesitation in attacking their version of the faith as a different gospel which was no gospel (see Gal. 1:6, 7).

The Council of Jerusalem was now beginning to reach a real consensus of opinion, but there was a remarkable contribution yet to be made by James, the Lord's brother. He referred the assembly back to the Old Testament Scriptures which constituted their whole Bible at that time. 'God . . . visited the Gentiles,' he said, 'to take out of them a people for his name. And with this the words of the prophets agree' (verses 14, 15). He then quoted the prophecy of Amos. His words were highly significant, for this was no casual quoting of a favourite proof-text out of context, in the manner of so many Christians when they disagree. It was the expression of a profound understanding of the whole tenor of Old Testament prophecy in the light of the contemporary working of the Holy Spirit. No doubt his radical interpretation of the inner meaning of the well-loved promises to Israel sprang from the teaching given by Jesus himself to his disciples when, as Luke tells us, 'beginning with Moses and all the prophets, he interpreted to them in all the scriptures the things concerning himself' (Lk. 24:27). It was in accord with the application of the prophetic message consistently employed by the other apostles. It linked the ancient promises boldly and firmly with the current activity of God.

Such an approach is precisely what is needed in the baptismal controversy. A prophetic view is needed, which can point out the sweep of God's purposes as revealed in Scripture and boldly apply it to the contemporary situation, in the light of what God is seen to be doing. Can the hand of the sovereign God not be seen in today's events: in the virtual disappearance of the old unreal 'Christendom'; in the emergence of the younger churches of Africa, Asia and

South America, eager to advance and impatient with old divisions inherited from alien cultures; in the division between church and secular state which is becoming so clear; in the forcing together through pressure and persecution of Christians once separated; in the remarkable working of God's Spirit in unexpected places? And does not the whole baptismal divide cry to be reconsidered in the light of these manifestations of the work of God, fulfilling the promises of his Word?

So the deliberations came to an end. The outcome must surely be called a working compromise. It maintained the essential nature of the gospel, but it asked Christians on either side of the dispute to make concessions to each other. Gentile Christians saw no reason to accept the ceremonial restrictions of the Jews on the eating of certain foods. Jewish Christians saw every reason for such restrictions. Moreover, they were not completely convinced that Gentile converts would be able and willing to make a clean break with the idolatry and immorality which permeated their world. The proposed compromise was that Jewish Christians, having accepted whole-heartedly that circumcision has no bearing on the essential nature of the gospel, should be able to expect Gentile converts to recognize their difficulties about certain foods. And, of course, they had every right to expect deeds to go with words when it came to conversion. 'Abstain from what has been sacrificed to idols and from blood and from what is strangled and from unchastity. If you keep yourselves from these, you will do well' (verse 29).

It was an arrangement which required forbearance and understanding from both parties. It asked Gentiles to give up more than was strictly required by the terms of the gospel, as Paul's later writings make clear (Rom. 14 and 1 Cor. 8). But it did so in order to preserve the greater unity. 'Let every one be fully convinced in his own mind. . . . Why do you pass judgment on your brother? . . . Decide never to put a stumbling block or hindrance in the way of a brother. . . . Let us then pursue what makes for peace. . . . Take care lest this liberty of yours somehow become a stumbling block to the weak. . . . Sinning against your brethren and wounding their conscience when it is weak, you sin against Christ' (Rom. 14:5, 10, 13, 19; 1 Cor. 8:9, 12).

The arrangement was an admirable one. It issued no rigid decrees, and was capable of very elastic application. 'A religious romanticist could not possibly have invented anything which left so much unsolved.'[1] Yet this was the decision which the apostles felt able to describe as having been made by 'the Holy Spirit and . . . us' (Acts 15:28). Can some similar solution be found to the baptismal controversy? Can a similar working compromise be reached which will preserve the essence of the gospel without destroying the vital emphases which both sides hold so dear because they express important aspects of that gospel? We believe it can, and we would humbly suggest that the way forward could lie along the following lines.

First, there must be a recognition of the principle of regenerate membership. The Christian church is made up of Christians. That needs to be said and heard, shown and seen. In today's almost universal situation of Christianity versus various types of paganism, there is a sense in which it has never been easier to demonstrate. Certainly, it has never been more urgently necessary. Having said that, it must frankly be accepted that there are still difficulties of definition and of application. Clearly, people can make a false profession of Christianity, for various reasons. Clearly, children may well be truly Christian before they can make a mature and adequate profession of faith. Clearly, the children of Christian homes are in a special position. In view of this, baptists must recognize that there will always be some Christians who will wish to baptize their children. Equally, paedobaptists must recognize that an indiscrimin-

[1] Farrar, *The life and work of St Paul* (Cassell, 1904), p. 245.

ate extension of baptism to all children debases the rite and scandalizes their brethren. Some paedobaptists are, of course, already urging a much greater degree of discipline on their fellows in the administration of baptism. Thus, Colin Buchanan (Church of England) has recently written, 'Indiscriminate infant baptism penalises the recipients of the rite. . . . The point of penalising is if and when youngsters from unbelieving homes ever become Christians. If so, it will be by genuine conversion, not by Christian upbringing. And if this is so, then the conversion should be marked, established and sealed by baptism. A new convert is most likely to need this point of no return provided in baptism, and has difficulty in understanding the value of a far past infant baptism which never brought him into actual relationship with God or his people.'[1] In similar vein John Baillie (Church of Scotland) has declared, 'It would therefore be a gross abuse of the sacrament if we should baptize babies who are not the children of Christian parents, who neither were born nor are to be brought up in a Christian home or within a Christian congregation. It is through his Christian nurture that the grace of God reaches the child – through the home into which he is born and the Christian community into which he is received. If he is not effectively received into such a community, if there is *nobody* who is caring for his Christian upbringing, then the outward ritual – the washing with water – *is not Christian baptism at all*, and means nothing.'[2] Would that more paedobaptist ministers would heed these warnings, in theory and in practice!

If a recognition of the principle of regenerate membership with all that it entails for a disciplined approach to paedobaptism is to be the first step on the way to reconciliation, an eschewal of confirmation for Christians already in good standing with other denominational churches must

[1] Buchanan, *Baptismal discipline*, p. 16.
[2] Baillie, *Baptism and conversion* (OUP, 1964), p. 44. Italics ours.

surely be the second. What possible advantage can confirmation be to a Baptist, a Pentecostal, a member of the Christian Brethren, wishing to join the Church of England? The promises made in confirmation have already been made in baptism. A serious and responsible approach to church membership has already been displayed. To make such a one now undergo a ceremony which is for him both meaningless and superfluous is to come close to following (in spirit at least) the Galatian heretics and the Judaizing opponents of the apostle Paul.

Of course, if paedobaptists are to be asked to give ground out of Christian love and respect for their baptist brethren, baptists themselves must willingly do the same. A softening of attitudes and a response of love and trust is similarly required of them too.

It is surely reasonable to ask for a frank admission that baptists do not have the right in every argument. There is no example in the New Testament of the baptism of an adult born of Christian parents – can that be frankly admitted? The children of Christian parents enjoy a state of privilege in several respects – can that be willingly conceded? Paedobaptists are deeply concerned to be loyal to the Scriptures, and believe themselves to be obeying the will of God when they baptize children – can that be openly acknowledged?

Following from this, is it not also reasonable to ask all baptists to relax their demand for rebaptism when admitting into their churches Christians *in good standing* with their own paedobaptist churches. Many, of course, already make such transfers of membership easy; cannot the remainder follow their example? If baptists would be excused confirmation they must likewise excuse rebaptism.

Happily, some baptists are responding to this challenge. More hard thinking is being done about the role of the child in the church, and about the slipshod definitions which too often accompany a boasted belief in 'regenerate membership' than has occurred for a long time. Thus, Stephen Winward has written, 'to define the church apart from the catechumenate (infants, children, youths, adults being disciplized) is to define her in static rather than dynamic terms'.[1] A document produced by the Baptist Union of Great Britain, *Baptists and unity*, has asked whether differences of judgment on baptism justify separation from other Christians, and has pointed hopefully to the increasing paedobaptist emphasis on faith as associated with baptism. But perhaps the most sweeping suggestion has come from a group who have produced another document, *Baptists for unity*. Admitting that a problem exists with no final solution, they have argued that the urgency of mission must have priority. Christians must work together while the problems are being solved. So they have advocated a temporary working arrangement, asking fellow baptists to recognize a complete initiation complex involving instruction, confession of faith, baptism and the laying-on-of-hands, *in any order*. It must be admitted in all fairness that these views are unrepresentative of the main body of baptist opinion, and that the final suggestion emanates from a group viewed with great suspicion by evangelicals for their 'radical' theology. Nevertheless, the signs of shifting opinion are evident, and very many evangelical baptists convey by their deeds, if not by formal declaration, their impatience with the whole area of division over baptism. Embarrassed when church rules demand rebaptism where they feel it inappropriate, they long for the day when unity in Christ finds the greater expression in practice that it already does in theory.

The Church of North India

If the day of practical Christian unity and intercommunion still seems, to many, to await the final coming of the

[1] Gilmore (Ed.), *The pattern of the church: a Baptist view* (Lutterworth, 1963), pp. 60, 61.

kingdom of God, it should not be forgotten that as recently as 1970 Anglicans, Methodists, Presbyterians, Congregationalists (all paedobaptists), Baptists, Churches of Brethren and Disciples of Christ (all baptists), formed together the United Church of North India and Pakistan. Their *Scheme of church union* is most instructive and relevant.

First, the principle of regenerate membership is laid down: 'Those are members . . . according to the will and purpose of God who are baptized into the Name of the Father, the Son and the Holy Spirit, receive the calling and grace of God with repentance and faith, and continue steadfast therein.'[1] It should be remembered that the insistence that the church is made up of Christians is basic to the baptist position. Because the majority of baptists in North India have been persuaded that this insistence is adequately met in the new scheme they have been able to join the new church.

Towards tomorrow

If, however, the Indian experiment is unlikely to be repeated in the West, contemporary developments are occurring here which equally highlight the need to resolve the baptismal problem. First, there are active negotiations with a view to union between the United Reformed Church (paedobaptist) and the Churches of Christ (baptist). It is fascinating and instructive to see how the subject of baptism has become the biggest stumbling-block to this scheme.

The Joint Committee Interim Report for 1975 contains twenty sections, of which ten are devoted to baptism. Out of six problems listed as urgently requiring solution, four are concerned with baptism. They revolve around the difficulty of holding two views of baptism in one congregation, the problem of a member baptized in infancy later asking for 'believers' baptism', and the prospect of

[1] *Scheme of church union in North India and Pakistan* (CLS, 1965), p. 2.

building both a font and a baptistry in each chapel of the uniting denominations. The Report proposes two principles which it frankly admits cannot be fully reconciled at present. 'What is theologically wrong cannot be pastorally right,'[1] but 'Any illogicality in this position is transcended by the deeper and more scandalous illogicality which allows us to recognize each other as fellow members of the Church and yet to stay apart in separate denominations.'[2] This pin-points the whole problem.

Already the issue has been highlighted in a much wider area too. The Churches' Unity Commission is pressing upon every major denomination the need to reach some decision on 'Ten Propositions for Visible Unity' made in 1976. This seems to represent a dramatic turning aside from previous schemes of organizational unity, towards a more informal expression of the inner unity already felt to exist between all true Christians. Proposition 5 suggests, 'From an accepted date, initiation in the covenanting Churches shall be by mutually acceptable rites.' Here is a grasping of the nettle indeed! Explanatory notes suggest a 'total process of initiation' in which 'the temporal order would not be unvarying'. In other words, baptism in water, laying-on-of-hands and confession of faith may be administered and accepted in various combinations and in any order. Immediate Baptist reaction has been, of course, to insist on freedom of conscience to accept and administer what others would regard as 'rebaptism'. The issues are being joined in the most practical and urgent manner.

Secondly, and at the other end of the spectrum, the charismatic movement has not only brought new currents of enthusiasm and an impatience with outworn forms, but has raised insistent new theological issues with its emphasis

[1] *The negotiations between Churches of Christ and the United Reformed Church*, Joint Committee Interim Report, 1975. Printed by Clare Son & Co. Ltd., p. 3.

[2] *Ibid.*, p. 4.

on the 'baptism of the Spirit'. Many claim that the objective reality of their believers' baptism or their confirmation has received only recent subjective expression in a new release of the Holy Spirit. As a consequence, the rites themselves have begun to hold a fading importance in their estimation. A recent charismatic book written by a Roman Catholic warns that there are 'dangers' in the movement, and mentions, among other things, a devaluation of the sacraments, a preoccupation with a Pauline and Wesleyan conversion experience and a tendency to seek rebaptism! Other charismatics have reacted differently, and are pressing for a whole new look at the sacraments in the light of their experience, claiming that this has deepened, not lessened, their regard for the sacraments. Yet others have impatiently thrown the whole of the past overboard, and it has not been unknown for the occasional Anglican vicar to arrange for adult baptisms and rebaptisms on a scale rarely seen by any of his baptist colleagues.

At another level the establishment of Christian witness in new towns and other new housing areas is bringing its own particular developments. Since buildings are expensive and churches are hard up, it is becoming increasingly common for the denominational churches to share one 'ecumenical centre' in these situations with an ostentatious font and baptistry displayed side by side. Yet surely this of itself is insufficient. It simply publicizes the division. New town situations should be more fully exploited.

One great advantage of the new town is the clarifying of the issues and the sharpening of the distinction between the church and the world, between the believer and the unbeliever. If the unashamed paganism of many such areas is grievous and shocking, it is at least realistic. The 'parish church' now caters for a minority group of committed worshippers as the nonconformist churches have always done. Baptism at six weeks and confirmation at fourteen years will never be the norm. Given a faithful ministry, the parish church congregation is likely to maintain, in practice if not in theory, a 'regenerate membership'. The clergyman is thus in a splendid position to cut down severely on the number of occasions when non-Christians bring their babies for baptism. He now has official sanction to offer a service of thanksgiving and blessing in place of baptism, a service, be it noted, which is little different from a baptist dedication service.

If the paedobaptist clergyman thus moves, perhaps unconsciously, to a position nearer to his baptist counterpart, cannot the baptist minister, for his part, join him in accepting some form of Christian household baptism, and thus himself move closer to the paedobaptist position? Household baptism is found in the New Testament, yet rarely in baptist experience. Does not the new town situation offer a unique opportunity for paedobaptists and baptists to work together in whole-hearted commitment to a form of evangelism which aims to win the family as a unit, and would not this be a welcome return to scriptural principles, pioneering the way for evangelism throughout the country into the twenty-first century? For too long evangelical Christians have been content to fill their churches with children who have streamed in at four and streamed out again at fourteen. Is it not now time to attempt to win the parents, that in turn whole families may be won for the faith? When this happens, household baptism – the baptism of believing parents and believing children together – becomes a beautiful reality instead of a mere phrase used as a weapon in the baptismal controversy.

If the new towns offer one way forward for the future, the 'house-church movement' may provide another. Where main-line denominational churches have died into nine-tenths empty buildings, designed for an earlier age, attended by a handful of discouraged and often ageing folk, starved of a biblical, Spirit-filled ministry, Christians with a living awareness of the power of Christ are finding themselves called to found new churches and to welcome all who share their experience, regardless of former denominational affiliation. Often meeting at first in the home of a member, sometimes acquiring another building later, such new groups are increasingly becoming an important feature of the British Christian scene, and whatever one's doubts about them, it must be admitted that some are engaged in strategic church-planting in unevangelized areas.

When any new church is formed, however, sooner or later the insistent question arises, What is to be done about baptism? Sadly, some of these new groups are merely perpetuating the old divisions and are either offending some who would join them, or more directly are turning them away. Others are rejecting baptism altogether, while still others claim to practise baptism in both kinds, without having thought out clearly the implications of what they are doing. Here again, as in the new towns, is a splendid opportunity for these new groups to direct their evangelistic efforts to the winning of whole families for Christ; an opportunity of allowing Christian parents to express positively their belief in the purpose of God for their children, and thus to transcend the baptismal differences which have divided Christians for so long.

Three hundred years have passed since John Owen and John Bunyan almost reached an accommodation on their differences in baptismal judgment.[1] May it be granted to the church at the end of the twentieth century to realize their noble vision, that all may say with the tinker of Bedford, 'I dare not have communion with them that profess not faith. . . . I am bold to hold communion with visible saints . . . because God hath communion with them. . . . Failure in such a circumstance as water, doth not unchristian us.'[2]

[1] See above, ch. 8.

[2] Bunyan, *A reason of my practice in worship*. Quoted in Offor, *The works of John Bunyan*, Vol. 2, pp. 602, 610, 611.

Select bibliography

Kurt Aland, *Did the early church baptize infants?*, English translation (SCM, 1963).
John Baillie, *Baptism and conversion* (Oxford University Press, 1964).
Baptists and unity (Baptist Union of Great Britain and Ireland, 1967).
Baptists for unity (Baptist Renewal Group, 1969).
Karl Barth, *The teaching of the church regarding baptism*, English translation (SCM, 1948).
G. R. Beasley-Murray, *Baptism in the New Testament* (Macmillan, 1963; reissued Paternoster Press, 1972).
G. R. Beasley-Murray, *Baptism today and tomorrow* (Macmillan, 1966).
Vera Brittain, *In the steps of John Bunyan* (Rich & Cowan, 1950; reissued R. West publishers, 1973).
E. H. Broadbent, *The pilgrim church* (Pickering & Inglis, 1935).
Colin O. Buchanan, *Baptismal discipline* (Grove Books, 1972).
Colin O. Buchanan, *A case for infant baptism* (Grove Books, 1973).
Jeffrey Burton, *Dissent and reform in the early Middle Ages* (Cambridge University Press, 1968).
C. H. B. Byworth, *Communion, confirmation and commitment* (Grove Books, 1972).
John Calvin, *Institutes of the Christian religion*, English translation (SCM, 1961).
Letters of C. A. Coates (Stow Hill Bible and Tract Depot).
The Commission on Christian Initiation, *Christian initiation, birth and growth in the Christian society*, commonly known as the Ely Report (Church Information Office, 1971).
Henry Cook, *What Baptists stand for* (Carey Kingsgate Press, 1947).
O. Cullmann, *Baptism in the New Testament*, English translation (SCM, 1950).
Arnold Dallimore, *George Whitefield* (Banner of Truth, 1970).
Dom Gregory Dix, *The theology of confirmation in relation to baptism* (Dacre Press, 1946).
J. D. Douglas (Ed.), *The new international dictionary of the Christian church* (Paternoster Press, 1974).
Ernest Evans, *Tertullian's homily on baptism* (SPCK, 1964).

Frederic Farrar, *The life and work of St Paul* (Cassell, 1904).
A. Gilmore (Ed.), *The pattern of the church: a Baptist view* (Lutterworth, 1963).
Bernard G. Holland, *Baptism in early Methodism* (Epworth, 1970).
Joachim Jeremias, *Infant baptism in the first four centuries*, English translation (SCM, 1960).
Joachim Jeremias, *The origins of infant baptism*, English translation (SCM, 1963).
Paul K. Jewett, *Infant baptism and confirmation*, copyright 1960, unpublished.
Joint Committees on Baptism, Confirmation and Holy Communion to the Convocations of Canterbury and York, *Baptism and confirmation today* (SPCK, 1955).
J. N. D. Kelly, *Early Christian doctrines* (A. & C. Black, second edn., 1960).
David Kingdom, *Children of Abraham* (Henry E. Walter Ltd., 1973).
J. K. F. Knaake (Ed.), *The works of Martin Luther* (Muhlenburg Press for Concordia, 1960).
G. W. H. Lampe, *The seal of the Spirit* (SPCK, 1967).
Kenneth Scott Latourette, *A history of the expansion of Christianity* (Eyre & Spottiswoode, 1954; reissued Paternoster Press, 1971).
Pierre Ch. Marcel, *The biblical doctrine of infant baptism*, English translation (James Clarke, 1953).
D. W. Marshall, *et al.*, *Approaches to the reformation of the church*, six papers given at the Puritan and Reformed Studies Conference, December 1965, published by *The evangelical magazine*.
Andrew Miller, *Church history* (G. Morrish, 1874–1879; reissued Pickering & Inglis, 1963).
John Murray, *Christian baptism* (Presbyterian & Reformed Publishing Co., 1962).
George Offor (Ed.), *The works of John Bunyan* (Blackie & Son, 1848).
John Owen, *Collected works* (Banner of Truth, 1965,6).
David Pawson & Colin Buchanan, *Infant baptism under cross-examination* (Grove Books, 1974).
Cyril F. Pocknee, *Water and the Spirit* (Darton, Longman & Todd, 1967).
E. Roberts-Thomson, *With hands outstretched* (Marshall, Morgan & Scott, 1962).
H. Wheeler Robinson, *Baptist principles* (Carey Kingsgate Press, 1935).
Scheme of church union in North India and Pakistan (Christian Literature Society, fourth revised edn., 1965).
J. Stevenson (Ed.), *A new Eusebius* (SPCK, 1960).
L. S. Thornton, *Confirmation: Its place in the baptismal mystery* (Dacre Press: A. & C. Black, 1954).
Leonard Verduin, *The reformers and their stepchildren* (Paternoster Press, 1964).
Thomas Watson, *The ten commandments* (Banner of Truth, 1962).
R. E. O. White, *The biblical doctrine of initiation* (Hodder & Stoughton, 1960).
G. H. Williams, *The radical reformation* (Weidenfeld & Nicolson, 1962).

Index

Abraham, 43–46, 50, 65
Anabaptist, 96–99, 103, 106–111, 113, 115–117, 119–122, 124, 125, 127, 128, 134, 148, 165
Anglicans, *see under* Church of England
Arminian, 140, 182
Augustine of Hippo, 37, 38, 82, 120, 182

Bakht Singh movement, 146
Baptism, believers', 11, 26, 55–70, 104, 131, 145–147, 165–171, 173
Baptism, household, 22, 29–31, 34, 47, 56, 57, 147, 203
Baptism, Jewish proselyte, 36, 48, 57
Baptism of Jesus, 15, 17, 19, 40, 41, 93
Baptism of John, *see under* John the Baptist
Baptism with the Holy Spirit, 17, 19–21, 23, 25, 27, 29, 41, 46, 53, 56, 69, 139–141, 158, 169, 192, 202
Baptist Union, 67, 166, 199
Baptists, 8, 11, 63, 66, 67, 92, 97, 128, 130–136, 142, 144, 145, 148, 150, 166, 171, 192, 198, 200, 201
Baptists, General, 127
Baptists, Particular, 127
Barbes, *see under* Waldensians
Baxter, Richard, 125
Brethren, Bohemian, 104
Brethren, Christian, 164, 198, 200
Brethren, Exclusive, 146, 147
Brethren, Open, 145
Brethren, Swiss, 87, 104, 117
Brown, John, 125
Bunyan, John, 125, 128, 131–136, 204

Calvin, John, 42, 54, 84, 90, 96, 97, 105, 112, 119–127, 135, 139, 140, 161, 182
Carey, William, 143
Carthage, 73
Catechumens, 78, 79
Charismatic movement, 201, 202
Church of England, 8, 42, 67, 97, 126, 128, 131, 132, 135, 138, 140, 141, 144, 148, 150, 160, 161, 189, 192, 197, 198
Church of Scotland, *see under* Presbyterian
Clark, Neville, 175, 176
Congregationalists, 127, 128, 144, 189, 200
Confirmation, 83–85, 157, 158, 161, 184, 189, 190, 202
Constantine, 77, 91
Cornelius, 20, 29, 34, 46, 56, 169
Covenant of grace, 42–44, 47, 61, 62, 64, 65, 134, 183
Covenant of law, 42–44, 61
Cromwell, Oliver, 126, 128, 129, 131
Crispus, 34, 57
Cyril of Jerusalem, 79, 80

Darby, J. N., 145, 146
Dissenters, 127, 131, 132, 135
Dix, Dom Gregory, 35, 158–160

Ecumenical Movement, 148–150
Edict of Milan, 77
Eunuch, Ethiopian, 22, 30, 55, 168
Exorcism, 76, 79, 80, 84

Gathered church, concept of, 66, 128
Geneva, 86, 89, 119, 126, 127
Gifford, John, 130–132
Grebel, Conrad, 104, 107

Hannah, 176, 177
Hippolytus, 75, 76, 78, 80, 159, 160
Hubmaier, Balthasar, 104

Independents, 97, 125, 130–132, 135
Infant dedication, 32, 174–179

Jeremias, Joachim, 35, 75
John the Baptist, 15–17, 19, 21, 24, 52, 53
Justin Martyr, 35, 75, 76, 78, 80

Keswick Convention, 149
Knox, John, 41

Little Flock, 146
Luther, Martin, 52, 53, 68, 89, 91, 99–101, 104, 106, 108–113, 119, 120
Lutherans, 91, 100, 103, 111, 112, 115, 118, 120
Lydia, 28, 30, 34, 170

Marcel, Pierre, 10, 42
Mary, mother of Jesus, 83, 177
Mass, 103, 108, 113
Mennonites, 113–118, 127
Methodism, 112, 138, 142, 144, 150
Müller, George, 145

Nicodemus, 25
Noah, 44, 45
Nonconformists, 141, 147
North India, Church of, 199, 200

Obberites, 117
Origen, 34, 57, 75
Original sin, 37, 38, 82, 89
Orthodox churches, 24, 25, 59, 91–93, 161

Paedobaptism, 25, 33–54, 82–85, 109, 120–123, 154–157, 162
Paul, 15, 20–24, 27, 30, 31, 34, 36, 37, 43, 47, 49, 51, 56, 57, 61–63, 73, 168, 169, 172, 174, 181, 190, 192–195, 198
Paulicians, 91–93, 175
Pelagian, 182
Pentecostals, 97, 146, 164, 189, 198
Peter, 19, 20, 27, 29, 46, 51, 57, 61, 66, 159, 168, 169, 192, 193
Philip, 22, 30, 55, 66, 167–169
Philippian goaler, 22, 30, 34, 47, 56, 77, 168, 170
Polycarp, 35, 57, 173
Presbyterian, 41, 97, 127, 130, 135, 138, 144, 197, 200
Protestants, 87–89, 92, 95–97, 103, 106, 107, 110, 119, 124, 135, 136, 144, 145, 148, 162, 164, 184, 192
Puritans, 10, 125, 126, 132, 137, 139

Radicals, 114–117, 119, 120, 124
Reformation, 10, 25, 26, 31, 42, 84, 85, 87–90, 94–99, 101, 102, 105, 111, 112, 124, 127
Reformed Churches of Geneva, *see under* Geneva
Rogers, William, 125
Roman Catholic Church, 24, 25, 59, 86–91, 100, 101, 105, 107, 108, 110, 115, 118, 120, 124, 135, 148, 189

Sacralism, Christian, 83, 85, 106, 126
Salvation Army, 7, 27
Samaritans, 21, 22, 66, 159, 167, 170
Silas, 22, 30, 168
Simons, Menno, 112, 113, 115–119
Smyth, John, 125
Sockler, Hans, 107
Spurgeon, Charles Haddon, 55, 56, 70, 147, 148, 180
Stephanas, 56
Stuart, royal family of, 126
Studd, C. T., 145

Taylor, J. Hudson, 145
Tertullian, 57, 73, 74, 81–83, 180
Thornton, L. S., 158–160
Tractarian Movement, 148
Titus, 20–22

Waldensians, 86–89, 120, 124
Waldo, Peter, 87, 90
Watson, Thomas, 125, 128, 129
Wesley, Charles, 138, 140–142
Wesley, John, 138, 140–142, 162
Wesleyan Methodists, *see under* Methodism
Whitefield, George, 138–140, 142, 162
Wittenberg, 102
World Council of Churches, 148, 149

Zaïre, 144
Zurich, 102, 104
Zwingli, Ulrich, 95, 96, 102–108, 120